City Going Up

A Journal of Exeter City F.C.

Season 1963/4

Mike Blackstone

Published by Rel8 Media

2013

City Going Up

Published by Rel8 Media

Unit 7, Woodend Business Centre, Cowdenbeath, Fife, KY4 8HG

© Rel8 Media and Mike Blackstone, 2013

All rights reserved. No part of this publication may be reproduced or copied an any manner without the permission of the copyright holders. A great deal of effort has been made to ensure that the information in this book is as accurate as possible. However, the publishers or authors cannot accept responsibility for any consequences arising from using this book.

The right of Mike Blackstone to be identified as the Author of this work has been asserted in accordance with the Copyrights, Designs and Patents Act, 1988.

Sources used have been credited where known. The author has tried to clear all copyright permissions but where this has not been possible and where amendments are required, then publisher will be pleased to make any necessary arrangements at the earliest opportunity.

British Library in Publication Data.

A catalogue record for this volume is available from the British Library.

ISBN 978-0-09574645-1-3

ABOUT THE AUTHOR

Although Mike Blackstone has lived the greater part of his life in Exmouth, Devon, for over ten years now he has resided 'up north' in a far flung corner of North West Lancashire, in Heysham, Morecambe.

Some 300 miles from his beloved St James' Park - home of Exeter City Football Club - he doesn't watch the team play now, but retains the same passion for recording the history of The Grecians as he did when he first set foot inside the 'Park' during the 1959-60 season.

An Exeter City statistician and programme collector, Mike started to contribute articles to the club's match programme in 1969 and became the editor of the publication during the 1992-93 season.

Having won a string of awards for the programme, several years in succession, including best programme in the country on more than one occasion, he stepped aside for the 2011-12 season.

He has contributed to numerous books, magazines, newspapers and programmes of many other clubs, and he is also the author of several books, prior to this one, as listed below.

His enthusiasm for the game, together with his love of reading and writing about it, as well as sampling real ales and enjoying photography in the North West shows no sign of diminishing.

Mike has two Blogs covering his other interests beer and photography, which are updated almost daily and can be found at:-

www.beerstagger.blogspot.co.uk
www.northwestimages.blogspot.co.uk

It is hoped that this book will become a record in what proved to be a memorable season in the history of Exeter City Football Club

ALSO BY MIKE BLACKSTONE

* Exeter City: A File Of Fascinating Football Facts. ISBN 0-946-65153-1. Obelisk Publications. 1992.
* Plymouth Argyle. A File of Fascinating Football Facts. ISBN 0-94665165-5. Obelisk Publications. 1993.
* The Brown Sauce Is off: A North West Non-League Odyssey. ISBN 0-954-82010-X. Mike Blackstone 2004.
* Exeter City F.C.: A Grecian Anthology. ISBN 978-0-9548201-1-4. Mike Blackstone. 2008
* Exeter City Down The Years. ISBN 978-09555307-9-1. Rel8 Media. 2012
* Exeter City F.C.: A to Z of Players. (awaiting publication)
* Exeter City: A Journal of the 1876-77 season (In preparation)

DEDICATION
To the management and players of Exeter City F.C. who created club history in the 1963-64 season.

To Lynda for her tremendous support and encouragement throughout the writing of this book.

ACKNOWLEDGEMENTS
I would like to thank everyone who has assisted in the writing of this book.

In particular to Grecians' legendary goalscorer, Alan Banks, for both the fond memories he has of the season which he was happy to share.

I would also like to thank Graham Rees, another member of the Exeter City squad in 1963/4, and long-serving player, for his own recollection of the promotion season.

Finally huge thanks to Andy McGregor of Rel8 Media Publishing for his support, suggestions and having faith in the project from day one.

SOURCES
Other than those already acknowledged elsewhere in the book, I have constantly referred to the written history of the Grecians which has appeared in various publications over the years.

Apart from my own comprehensive records of the club, I would like to mention the following publications etc., all which have been of tremendous value in writing this book:-

Express and Echo newspaper, Exeter.
Western Morning News newspaper, Plymouth.
The P.F.A. Premier & Football League Players' Records 1946-2005. Barry Hugman. Queen Anne Press.
Exeter City: A Complete Record 1904-1990 - Breedon Books
Match programmes from games played by Exeter City throughout the 1963-64 season.

INTRODUCTION

Was it really 50 years ago that the Grecians won promotion for the first time in the club's history

The Exeter City side of 1963-64 may not have been the greatest football team ever seen, but they all stuck together, worked for one another and gave 100 per cent.

Built on the rock solid defence which usually lined up Alan Barnett, Cecil Smyth, Les MacDonald, Arnold Mitchell, Keith Harvey and Des Anderson, very few opposing teams found a way through the rearguard.

As a result, only Gillingham, also promoted that season, had a better defensive record. City eventually conceded just 37 goals in their 46 league matches played. The Gills conceded 30.

The crucial point of turning what was becoming a good season into an excellent one was surely when Alan Banks arrived at the club.

What a master stroke of a signing that proved to be. Signed from Cambridge City and a player who is still very much part of the Grecians' matchday scene attending home matches at St James' Park.

Making his debut in a 2-1 defeat at Tranmere Rovers on October 28 1964, just across the Mersey from his former Liverpool home, Banks didn't take long to get his name on the scoresheet.

His first goal came in a 2-0 win at Oxford United and he netted in four of the next five matches. With 18 goals in 28 starts, Banks easily topped the club's goalscoring charts as he was to do so again over the next few seasons.

His and the team's achievement was never better summed up than by that iconic photograph showing a banner stating: "Thanks to Banks and all the ranks."

The photograph was taken when the players arrived at Exeter St David's after playing at Workington and clinching promotion in the final match of the season.

Although the forward line was not as settled as the defence, the mainstays were Graham Rees, Alan Banks, Dermot Curtis, Derek Grace and Adrian Thorne.

We must also not forget the contributions made by the likes of Roy Patrick, John Henderson, John Edgar, George Spiers, John Cochrane, George Ley, Peter Phoenix, Peter Rutley, George Northcott, Dave Hancock and Jimmy Parkhill, all of whom helped the Grecians to that memorable first ever success.

They are players whom I can still visualise very clearly, even though it is 50 years ago. Can I do that with the promotion-winning City players of 1990? No I can't. Time does play tricks.

The 1963-64 City team was first one that I ever saw that brought success. Having attended my first game at St. James' Park at the end of the 1959-60 campaign, I then had to endure three seasons of struggle until promotion came along.

I therefore felt it was fitting that the achievements of the 1963-64 season should be suitably recorded with this book, which I have greatly enjoyed compiling.

It is in a diary format, detailing all the matches played, both by the first team and the reserves. All line ups for the latter have been included where we have been able to track them down.

League tables are included, so as to chart the progress of the team as the season unfolded.

To give flavour of the time, advertisements have also been reproduced which appeared in the Exeter City programme.

I hope you have as much enjoyment reading it, and recalling a truly great season that I for one, shall always remember.

Standing, back row: Jack Edwards (Manager), Keith Harvey, Cecil Smyth, Alan Barnett, Dave Hancock, Les MacDonald, Des Anderson.
Sitting, front row: Dermot Curtis, Arnold Mitchell, Adrian Thorne, Graham Rees, Derek Grace, Alan Banks.

Friday 17th May 1963

JACK EDWARDS APPOINTED TEAM MANAGER
Jack Edwards, the 33-year-old former Crystal Palace and Rochdale player, who came to St James' Park as trainer at the start of the 1962-63 season has been appointed manager of Exeter City.

Edwards, who had to take over the team, as well as continuing all the training duties on his own when Cyril Spiers left the club in February 1963, brought the team out of trouble from the bottom to the middle of the Fourth Division table.

He was not only a popular manager amongst players and supporters, but Edwards was much respected by all concerned, bringing success to the playing side of the Club.

City's Board of Directors unanimously confirmed his appointment at last night's board meeting at a salary of £1,040 per year.

Several names were linked with the job after Spiers left, but the appointment of Jack Edwards will be welcomed by most supporters.

FOXHAYES BECOME A NURSERY CLUB
Exeter City have taken a step towards strengthening the club's youth policy by adopting the twelve team Foxhayes F.C. soccer group as a nursery club.

Foxhayes have already produced goalkeeper Tony Clark, full-back Peter Quarrington and forward Alan Riding for City.

NEW SCOUT CONFIRMED
A Bristol-based scout, Mr. R. Preece has been appointed by Exeter City on the usual terms offered by the club to those in similar positions.

He would therefore be paid £50 when a player introduced by him makes his Football League debut and a further sum of £200 after the player has made 15 league appearances.

CITY MAKE OFFER FOR IRISH PLAYER
Exeter City have made an offer to Irish League club, Crusaders, for the transfer of George Spiers.

The Grecians have offered a fee of £150, plus 25% of any fee received should the player be transferred from Exeter City to another club in the future.

Friday 24th May 1963

EXETER CITY: EIGHT PLAYERS FOR TRANSFER
Exeter City have sacked eight of their 20-strong professional staff. Wingers Brian Jenkins and Jack McMillan are the only two players up for sale. The other six are available on free transfers.

City are asking for a fee of £1,500 for Jenkins and £1,000 for McMillan.

All those players given free transfers were brought to the club by former manager Cyril Spiers.

The retained list is as follows:-
Goalkeeper: Colin Tinsley.
Full-Backs: Les MacDonald, Roy Patrick, Cecil Smyth.
Half-Backs: Des Anderson, Derek Grace, Keith Harvey, Arnold Mitchell.
Forwards: Ray Carter, Graham Rees, Eric Welsh, John Henderson.

For Sale are:- Brian Jenkins, Eric McMillan
Free transfers:- Tony Clark, David Johnston, Mike Hughes, Barry Pierce, Charlie Sells, Ray Southcombe.

Meanwhile former Exeter City inside-forward, Archie Blue, has been given a free transfer by Carlisle United today.

He spent one season at St James' Park being signed from Hearts, before linking up with Carlisle last summer.

Thursday 30th May 1963

CITY SNIPPETS
Exeter City are to contact Wolverhampton Wanderers requesting why they gave trials to two players, Flowers and Hartnell.

This was despite being previously advised by the Grecians secretary that both are registered as amateurs at Exeter City.

Meanwhile good news, was that the supporters' group, the Grecians Association have donated £900 to Exeter City F.C.

The full Exeter City board of directors, plus manager Jack Edwards and club secretary Keith Honey, are to attend the Annual General Meeting of The Football League in London.

British Railways are to be asked for a copy of the 1921 agreement regarding rental of land, to enable full consideration to be given to their request for repair of fencing bordering St James' Park and adjacent the railway embankment.

Wednesday 5th June 1963

CITY SNIPPETS
Former Exeter City forward, Barry Pulman, has signed for Barnstaple Town, having played for Bridgwater Town during the 1962-63 season.

Pulman had four years with Exeter, two of them as a full professional, before moving into the Southern League, first with Margate, and then Trowbridge Town.

It was decided that Exeter City Residential Properties Limited be requested to arrange for all their houses to be valued by Estate Agents, Leslie Fulford.

It was the club's wish to replace the properties with more up to date housing for the use of players.

Wednesday 12th June 1963

RAY CARTER QUITS CITY
Exeter City's leading goalscorer will not be re-signing for the club next season. Ray Carter is quitting League football for the security of a house and a job in a sports shop.

The 30-year-old forward has emphasised that he is not in dispute with Exeter City, but the job he has been offered in Crawley will give himself and his family the security a player of his age is looking for.

He hopes to play for Southern League side, Crawley Town, as a part time professional.

Carter joined Exeter from Torquay United in October 1960 and finished as the club's leading goalscorer last season with 19 goals.

He has had a most unusual career for a footballer, for he was an office worker playing for Crawley Town as an amateur until he turned professional at the age of 25 for Torquay United.

Now after just five years in football, he has decided to return to Sussex and resume his playing career with Crawley Town.

Exeter City will continue to hold his Football League registration and have placed a fee of £7,500 on the player should he wish to sign for another League club.

Thursday 13th June 1963

CITY SNIPPETS
Another Exeter City player has the chance to follow Ray Carter into non-league football. This time it is former Cardiff City winger Brian Jenkins, who is on the club's

transfer list at £1,500.

Two clubs, Barnstaple Town and Chelmsford City, have now offered him terms, Neither club would pay a fee for the player should he decide to join one of them, as that only applies if he moves to another Football League club.

Former Reading and Exeter City inside-forward Tom Wilson, last season with Bridgwater Town, has been appointed player-manager of Somerset Senior League club, Street. The club have made an application to join the Western League.

Exeter City apprentice full-back, Peter Quarrington, is likely to accept the terms offered to become a full professional for the 1963-64 season.

Wing-half Des Anderson had requested a new two-year playing contract with the Grecians, however, the City board of directors could not agree to this.

Friday 14th June 1963

TRIALIST AND AMATEURS FOR THE GRECIANS
Exeter City are to give Bristol City's transfer listed inside-forward Adrian Williams a two-month trial.

They have also signed three amateurs, all from the Bristol area. Merlyn Jeremiah is an inside-forward who had previously played for Corinthian Casuals. Colin Weaver is a 15-year-old goalkeeper, and half back Malcolm Baker, is 21.

Friday 21st June 1963

CITY OFFER APPRENTICES A CONTRACT
Exeter City have offered full time professional contracts to apprentices, Peter Quarrington and Peter Rutley, both a year before their apprentice contracts expire.

Rutley is understood to be unhappy with the terms he has been offered. He has already made several appearances in City's first team.

Quarrington, who has yet to make a first team outing, is keen to sign the contract he has been offered.

CITY WANT £7,500 FOR CARTER
The Exeter City Board of Directors have decided to place a £7,500 transfer fee on the head of inside-forward Ray Carter, who has decided not to re-sign next season, and is to join Southern League Crawley Town.

The Board felt that it was not an unreasonable fee, as they did not want Carter to leave the club, having City's leading goal scorer for the past two seasons.

It would not prevent him from playing for Crawley as non league clubs do not have to pay nay kind of fee.

It is just a safeguard should Crawley ever sell the player, or he wanted to return to League football.

Thursday 27th June 1963

CITY SNIPPETS
Having received a transfer request from Derek Grace, the Exeter City board of directors decided not to accept it, the player having been retained for the 1963-64 season.

Half-back Des Anderson requested a free transfer, having previously asked for a two-year contract which was not agreed to. Once again it was decided that as Anderson had been retained and offered a deal for the forthcoming season, that his request could not be granted.

Tuesday 2nd July 1963

TINSLEY TURNS DOWN CITY OFFER
Colin Tinsley, Exeter City's only retained professional goalkeeper, has turned down a years contract which the club have offered him and he will continue to do so until City help him with his housing problem.

Tinsley, who joined the Grecians from Darlington two seasons ago, said that he had been in a club flat and a club house since then, neither of which suited him or his family.

He is therefore only signing monthly contracts until City solve his grievances.

Meanwhile, both apprentices offered full professional contracts have signed. They are Peter Quarrington and Peter Rutley.

All the players who had been retained by Exeter City, except for Des Anderson, Derek Grace and Les MacDonald, have now agreed terms and re- signed for the 1963-64 season.

BRISTOL ROVERS SIGN JENKINS
Brian Jenkins, the left-winger who was transfer listed by Exeter City for £1,500, has today signed for Bristol Rovers on a free transfer.

When his old contract expired last Sunday, City decided to give Jenkins a free transfer and Rovers moved in quickly to snap him up.

Jenkins had also received offers from Coventry City, Newport County, Torquay United, Barnstaple Town and Chelmsford City.

The 25-year-old player had joined the Grecians two years ago from Cardiff City.

Wednesday 3rd July 1963

McMILLAN NOT FOR TORQUAY UNITED
Jack McMillan, the right-winger who was placed on the transfer list by Exeter City for a £1,000 fee, lost a chance of signing for Torquay United because he was too honest.

Torquay manager Eric Webber wanted Jack to sign and play on the left wing, but the player said that he would be out of position completely on the left, so Torquay decided to look elsewhere.

Thursday 4th July 1963

CITY SNIPPETS
The main grandstand at St James' Park is to be re-roofed, with local company Redheugh-Willey being contracted to undertake the work.

Exeter City made enquiries with regards to signing Northampton Town half-back Barry Cooke. The former England youth international had previously played for West Bromwich Albion.

Adrian Williams has been signed from Bristol City on a two-month trial basis. The England schools and youth international inside-forward had made four league appearances for the Ashton Gate club since he signed a full professional contract in August 1960.

Des Anderson has now signed a new contract for Exeter City, whilst Derek Grace is on a month to month contract. Goalkeeper Colin Tinsley is also on a monthly contract until the issue with regards the players' housing is resolved.

Former apprentice half-back, Peter Rutley, has signed on a full professional contract.

Discussions took place about winding up club subsidiary company, Exeter Residential Properties Limited. At the same time it was agreed to put one of the club houses up for sale at 1 St. Sidwells Avenue, Exeter.

Friday 5th July 1963

TWO PLAYERS SIGN FOR CITY
Exeter City manager Jack Edwards made his first signings for the club by securing the services of former Portsmouth and Grimsby Town goalkeeper, Alan Barnett, and

former Barnsley, Gillingham, York City and Hartlepool inside-forward, John Edgar.

Both players are 27-years-old, but Barnett is the real capture of the two.

After two seasons with Portsmouth, where he made 30 appearances for them in the First Division, Barnett was signed by Grimsby Town and in his four years there had 147 first team outings.

Barnett was listed for a fee of £3,000 at the end of last season, but a talk between City vice chairman George Gillin and the Grimsby club chairman brought Barnett to St James' Park for only his accrued share of benefit.

After leaving Barnsley when he was 22, Edgar became leading scorer at all his next three clubs, with 24 goals at Gillingham, 16 at York City and 20 at Hartlepool.

He has had cartilage trouble, but the City have signed him following a check by the club doctor.

Thursday 11th July 1963

CITY SNIPPETS
Alvan Williams, the big-bearded centre-half, son of a parson, who played for Exeter City three seasons ago has applied for the manager / coach vacancy at Fourth Division Hartlepools.

He left City on a free transfer and took a player-managers post with a Cheshire League side. Williams is a qualified F.A. coach and is favourite for the Hartlepool job.

Unable to resolve the housing problem with goalkeeper Colin Tinsley, it was announced that the player would be granted a free transfer when his present contract ran out on 31st July.

The club had received permission to use the Royal Marines ground at Lympstone for practice matches.

Friday 12th July 1963

MacDONALD ASKS FOR A TRANSFER
Newcastle-born full-back Les MacDonald who has been with Exeter City for six years wants to go on the transfer list, although the club do not want him to go. He is only signing monthly contracts at the moment.

MacDonald lost the left-back spot in City's team towards the end of last season with the signing of Roy Patrick from Southampton.

He says he cannot see much future at Exeter City and does not want to spend another season in the reserve team.

MacDonald has met with the City Board of Directors, but they have been unable to persuade him to stay at St. James' Park.

Thursday 18th July 1963

TIME RUNNING OUT FOR CITY
With exactly a week to go before the professionals report back for training with Exeter City, the players position is worse than it was at the beginning of the summer.

They have signed just two players, Alan Barnett and John Edgar, but have lost two of the retained players, Colin Tinsley and Ray Carter.

In addition Les MacDonald is unsettled at the club and is only on a monthly contract. City have just four recognised forwards on the staff.

TWO GRECIANS FIND NEW CLUBS
Two Exeter City players have found new clubs for next season. Jack McMillan has signed for Southern League Margate on a free transfer.

inside-forward Charlie Sells who joined the Grecians last summer from Queen's Park Rangers has also agreed to go to a Southern League side, Guildford City.

Friday 19th July 1963

IRISH INTERNATIONAL SIGNS FOR CITY
Exeter City have signed a young Irish amateur international goalkeeper on a one month trial from Cliftonville, of Belfast.

He is Jim Parkhill, who played in every match last season for the Northern Ireland amateur international team.

He is 6' 1" tall and weighs 12 stone 7lbs, and becomes the second keeper to be signed by City this summer.

Tuesday 23rd July 1963

GRECIANS' ASSOCIATION MEMBERSHIP DRIVE
The Grecians' Association, Exeter City's supporters club, are starting a new membership drive which looks like taking their numbers up by several thousand.

Grecians' chairman, and City director, Les Kerslake, said they are circulating an entirely new form of membership card, which will entitle members to take part in a weekly football competition for a cash prize. The early indications are that the scheme will be a success.

Wednesday 24th July 1963

CITY PLAYERS REPORT BACK
Exeter City's manager had 15 professionals and three apprentices to work with when the players reported back for their new season. By the following week there should be several more.

If the Board of Directors can bring off the signings they are attempting, the senior staff should finish up about 20 strong.

New faces this morning were Alan Barnett, John Edgar and Adrian Williams on a two-month trial from Bristol City.

With the rest of the City staff they were kitted out by Jack Edwards and will be going to one of the city sports shops to choose their own new boots.

Training sessions started in the afternoon, when the City players were met by chairman, Reg Rose, and directors, Jack Rodgers and Les Kerslake for an informal get together.

Edwards would be assisted in training sessions by senior professionals, Arnold Mitchell and Keith Harvey.

Thursday 25th July 1963

CITY SNIPPETS
Exeter City sold two of their club houses, located at 1 St. Sidwells Avenue, for the sum of £2,450, and one at 12 West Terrace for £2,200.

Arnold Mitchell and Les MacDonald were to represent Exeter City FC and play in the annual Professional Footballers Golfers Association Championships.

Monday 29th July 1963

IRISHMEN ARRIVE AT CITY
Two more Irish players arrived in Exeter to start training with the rest of the staff.

Both are Irish amateur internationals. Jimmy Parkhill, a goalkeeper and John Symington, inside forward, who has schoolboy and youth caps. Symington was 17, and Belfast born,.

Both players were joining City on trial, as was 17-year-old George Ley, a left winger who was with Hitchin Town and Arsenal.

Wednesday 31st July 1963

GRANDSTAND ROOF
Work starts this week on a several thousand pound, three month job at St James' Park, the re-roofing of the entire Exeter City grandstand.

This is a job that the club has been postponing for years, but the roof has been getting worse and worse, and the work became vital this summer when a six foot piece of guttering came crashing down on to the running track.

Thursday 1st August 1963

TINSLEY FOR LUTON TOWN
Colin Tinsley, 27, the goalkeeper given a free transfer by Exeter City just three weeks ago, has agreed to sign for Third Division, Luton Town.

He made 44 appearances last season after joining City from Darlington two years ago. He has also received offers from Oxford United and Romford.

Friday 2nd August 1963

BIGGEST PROFIT SINCE THE WAR
Exeter City F.C. in their annual balance sheet issued today show that the club made a profit of £7,569 on the years working, only their second profit since the War and by far the largest.

The reason for the sudden change of fortune has been the gigantic increase in revenue from the Grecians Associations' Red and White Club, and the development fund lottery. This has shot up from £8,950 in 1961-62 to £23,264 in the current year.

The club's total deficiency has dropped from £42,635 to £35,066. The club spent only £2,000 on two players, John Henderson and Roy Patrick.

The money for re-roofing the grandstand has been guaranteed by the Grecians Association.

City chairman, Reg Rose is confident that the club will do well financially again this year with the aid of careful budgeting.

Gate receipts dropped from £12,758 to £12,114. Season tickets were down from £3,106 to £2,880.

Wages increased from £21,365 to £28,070, and travelling expenses went up by £800 to £4,882. A total of £3,100 was received in transfer fees.

IPSWICH TOWN FORWARD SIGNS
Exeter City have signed the top player that they have been chasing since director Les Kerslake made a flight to Ireland a month ago. He is Dermot Curtis, a 30-year-old Eire international centre-forward from First Division, Ipswich Town. City have paid a £1,000 fee for Curtis who was retained by Ipswich at the end of last season.

Born in Dublin, Curtis came to this country seven years ago to sign for Bristol City.

After two seasons he was transferred to Ipswich and has scored 17 goals in 41 League games there. He will continue to live and train in Ipswich for the time being. He is eager to move to Exeter to live as soon as possible as he likes this part of the country very much.

Saturday 3rd August 1963

ARBURY SIGNS APPRENTICE FORMS
Peter Arbury, the young full-back from Ottery St Mary, who was a member of the City team that did so well in the F.A. Youth Cup last season, has been signed as an apprentice professional.

Friday 9th August 1963

TWO TRIALISTS FOR CITY
Exeter City are giving a one-month trial to John Cochrane, a 19-year-old inside-forward who has been in Third Division football with Brighton and Hove Albion.

Born in Belfast, he joined Brighton two years ago. Last season he made 14 appearances scoring four goals. He was top scorer in their Football Combination side.

Meanwhile winger George Ley, has been signed initially on amateur forms, and will also have a one month trial at the club.

Tuesday 13th August 1963

FIRST FRIENDLY ENDS IN A DEFEAT
Weymouth 1 Exeter City 0
City team (starting line up): Barnett, Smyth, Patrick, Mitchell, Harvey, Anderson, Welsh, Cochrane, Henderson, Symington, Rees.

Exeter City still need forwards, inside forwards. This was the lesson they learned at Southern League. Weymouth. Despite changes in attack at the start of the second half, the craft to get goals was just not there.

The team tried hard enough, but the inside forwards lacked the experience to make the right sort of openings, or to take the strain off the defence for any length of time.
The defence played well, but the side that took to the field is unlikely to be anything

like the one that will play in the opening fixture of the season.

John Edgar was absent with a knee injury and Dermot Curtis is still in Ipswich. With these two in the team there should be a tremendous amount of difference which will also give a helping hand to the youngsters in the side.

Thursday 15th August 1963

PIERCE FOR SALISBURY
Former Exeter City inside-forward Barry Pierce has signed for Salisbury City.

Liverpool-born, Pierce signed for the Grecians from York City last July with the reputation as a goalgetter, but although he made 28 first team appearances, he never found his scoring touch and was given a free transfer at the end of last season.

Saturday 17th August 1963

CURTIS NETS HAT-TRICK
Reds 4 Whites 1
Reds team: Barnett (Parkhill), Smyth, MacDonald, Mitchell (Grace), Patrick (Mitchell), Anderson, Cochrane, Henderson, Curtis, Edgar, Rees.
Whites team: Parkhill (Barnett), Quarrington, Arbury (Guild), Rutley, Parsons, Grace (Allen), Stuckey, Redwood, Riding, Williams, Ley (Kirkpatrick).
Scorers: Reds: Curtis 3, Cochrane: Whites: Riding.
All the substitutions were made at half-time.

The Reds, a potential first team, didn't have any kind of test with the Whites consisting of a side of youngsters, mostly teenagers, including three trialists from a Dunfermline amateur club, namely, Allen, Guild and Kirkpatrick.

Though they looked a promising bunch, they could not provide anything like the sort of opposition which the City will meet at Bradford on Saturday, It does look as if the Grecians have made improvements where they needed them, mostly in attack.

Dermot Curtis showed with three quickly taken goals (7th, 55th and 75th minutes) that he is a bustler, a scorer and a constant danger. John Edgar showed that he can hold the ball when it is necessary and use it well.

It looks as if City may have found themselves another first team man in trialist, John Cochrane.

He was always dangerous and scored in the 69th minute. He impressed with his ability to beat a man and his direct approach.

There was promise shown by the Whites side. Alan Riding scored their only goal five minutes from time, but there was certainly not enough experience for the Fourth Division, with the exception of Derek Grace, who seems to have improved greatly since joining Exeter.

Tuesday 20th August 1963

CITY SIGN TWO MORE
Exeter City have signed two new players, former Torquay United centre-half George Northcott, 27, and 21-year-old utility player, George Spiers.

Northcott was consistently Torquay's centre-half until he had a knee injury about 18-months ago. When he could not get back into the first team he asked for a transfer and was listed for £5,000.

Instead of waiting for a League club he joined Southern League Cheltenham Town last season and arrives at St James' Park for a fee of £500.

Exeter had first discussed the possibility of signing Northcott three months ago, but a decision was deferred at the time.

Spiers comes from Irish League club, Crusaders. City have been negotiating for him for some time, and agreement was finally reached over the transfer fee yesterday.

City will pay a fee of £500 plus Crusaders will receive 25% of any future fee that Exeter may receive on the transfer of the player.

Spiers is reported to be an extremely strong, young player and can play at wing-half or inside-forward.

Saturday 24th August 1963

League Game 1
Saturday 24th August 1963
Valley Parade
Att 4668

Bradford City	1 v 2	Exeter City
Fisher	1	Barnett
Kelly	2	Smyth
Ellam	3	Patrick
Stowell	4	Mitchell
Smith	5	Harvey
Harland	6	Anderson
Hall	7	Rees
Wragg	8	Henderson(2)
Green(1)	9	Curtis
Price	10	Edgar
Thorpe	11	Spiers

CITY OFF TO A GOOD START

The Grecians gave a brilliant display at Valley Parade. It was a hard workmanlike performance in which Jack Edwards plan of "when you are playing away, defend and be patient, until you get the other side rattled into making mistakes, then pounce," was carried out perfectly.

John Henderson got the goals in the 55th and 65th minutes with Dermot Curtis helping him to forge both of them.

John Edgar seemed to be what City have been looking for in the way of a link man, whilst George Spiers, although he didn't make too much of an impression, did provide the cross that led to the first goal.

Most of the work in this game fell on the defence. They got a pounding for 70% of the match, but they held out until three minutes from time, when Green hammered in an 18-yard shot.

The plan meant a lot of running and covering and no one worked harder in this respect than Des Anderson, but the safest man on show was Alan Barnett.

His handling was clean and he made two magnificent saves that certainly kept the game from turning in Bradford's favour.

For Bradford were a side that did not give up, even though they went two goals down.

Western League
Exeter City 5 Portland United 2
Scorers: Exeter City: Redwood 2, Williams, Ley, Own-goal.
Exeter City team: Parkhill, Quarrington, MacDonald, Rutley, Parsons, Grace, Cochrane, Symington, Redwood, Williams, Ley
Portland United team: Morris, Warren, Hoskins, Caswell, Wilkes, Way, Stroud, Hollings, Bowring, House, McDonald.

Monday 26th August 1963

McILMOYLE GIVES CITY THE RUNAROUND

League Game 2
Monday 26th August 1963
Brunton Park
Att 6454

Carlisle United	3 v 0	**Exeter City**
Dean	1	Barnett
Neill	2	Smyth
Caldwell	3	Patrick
Oliphant	4	Mitchell
Marsden	5	Harvey
McDonnell	6	Anderson
Lornie	7	Rees
McIlmoyle (3)	8	Henderson
Livingstone	9	Curtis
Davies	10	Edgar
Kirkup	11	Spiers

There was one simple reason for Exeter City's beating, Carlisle United were just too good for them.

As they trudged miserably out of the midsummer monsoon which had lashed then almost throughout the game, City had to be thankful they had not gone down by six or seven goals.

Almost everyone in the City team hit a bad patch at the same time and Carlisle were too good a side not to take advantage of it.

The man who really tormented Exeter, was Hugh McIlmoyle, darting, thrusting and probing his way in and around the defence. He

SWITCH TO ELECTRIC HEATING WITH ECONOMY
OIL FILLED RADIATORS — NIGHT STORE HEATER
UNDER FLOOR HEATING

ROBERT BATEY & CO., LTD.,
109-111 LOWTHER STREET, CARLISLE

Home Heating Specialists   Telephone 21254/5.

CARLISLE UNITED FC

v.

EXCTER CITY

Nº 340

MONDAY, 26th AUG., 1963.

7-30 p.m. **KICK OFF**

PROGRAMME 3d

FOOTBALL LEAGUE

HOWE OF BRAMPTON
LIMITED
FOR THE
BEST IN PRINT
Tel.: BRAMPTON 447.

got all three goals in the 10th, 65th and 77th minutes.

Carlisle were a very good side. They moved intelligently and quickly with the ball, and they snapped hungrily at every scoring possibility.

In the 40th minute John Henderson cracked in a shot which Dean did well to push out, but apart from that City never looked like scoring.

The inside forwards and wingers were so ineffective that a lot of the Carlisle danger came from their defence who had the space to move up into attack.

The City plan fell to pieces because the team could never settle down to it. For most of the first half, the forwards did not receive a decent pass.

Wednesday 28th August 1963

Western League
Exeter City 0 Bridgwater Town 2
Scorers: Bridgwater: Thomas, Henderson.
Exeter City team: Parkhill, Quarrington, MacDonald, Northcott, Parsons, Grace, Stuckey, Riding, Redwood Rutley, Ley.

Friday 30th August 1963

CITY F.C. WERE ON THE BRINK OF FOLDING
At last night's meeting of shareholders, City F.C. Chairman Reg Rose said that as a businessman he had never seen or heard of a business in a worse mess than when he took over at St James' Park.

The club was at rock bottom and it had been touch and go whether to carry on, but he spoke of more settled times ahead. Things were getting a little easier and the Board of Directors could be more tolerant.

Team manager Jack Edwards told the ten shareholders present that there were players on the staff last season that did not give 100% on the field.

These players were no longer with the club and he guaranteed that any player who did not show commitment this season would be released. He also said that Exeter City will do much better than last season.

At the same meeting, club directors Jack Rodgers and Les Kerslake were re-elected to the Board.

Saturday 31st August 1963

League Game 3
Saturday 31st August 1963
St James Park
Att 5449

Exeter City	0 v 0	**Lincoln City**
Barnett	1	Carling
Smyth	2	Jones
Patrick	3	Smith
Mitchell	4	Linnecor
Harvey	5	Howard
Anderson	6	Neal
Cochrane	7	Holmes
Henderson	8	Morton
Curtis	9	Campbell
Rees	10	Rooney
Spiers	11	Bannister

STALEMATE AT THE PARK

This was a fair performance to get a point after carrying left-back Roy Patrick for the whole of the second half with a back injury.

John Cochrane showed plenty of promise and most of City's danger came from his direction.

Graham Rees turned in the hardest performance of the day and was unlucky not to get a couple of goals.

The City defence needs no improvement on this showing. Lincoln had plenty of potential danger in their forward line, but they were not allowed to show it.

Three men deserve particular praise. Cecil Smyth who seems to get better every game. Keith Harvey as cool as ever and Des Anderson, who so capably took over the left-back spot when Patrick was injured.

With Lincoln so bottled up, the game really boiled down to a question of if and when City would score.

They made quite a few chances, but their finishing was not so hot. The three really good efforts that were put in were all saved.

John Henderson had a shot deflected just wide. Rees had a drive stopped by a flying Carling dive, and a Dermot Curtis header was blocked by a very acrobatic effort from the Lincoln keeper.

Perhaps new forwards would mean new finish and that is what City need now.

Western League
Chippenham Town 1 Exeter City 0
Scorer: Chippenham: Not known.
Chippenham Town team: Webb, Steel, Perry, Beaven, Bollinger, May, Adams, Akers, Brownhall, Giles, Watkins.
Exeter City team: Parkhill, Quarrington, McDonald, Northcott, Parsons, Grace, Stuckey, Riding, Redwood, Rutley, Ley.

WHAT ARE THE PROSPECTS FOR CITY?

Everyone, of course, is wondering what is in store for Exeter City in these next eight months, but football being such an unpredictable game that it is often difficult to forecast the result of even one match, then it is obviously impossible to look very far into the future.

While it is generally admitted that City still need one or two more experienced forwards so that each position is covered in case of injuries.

There is no doubt that the club has done well with the limited number of signings that have been made.

Dermot Curtis has as much international experience as any other player in the Fourth Division.

Goalkeeper Alan Barnett has appeared in both the First and Second Divisions, whilst inside forward John Edgar has topped the scoring lists of three different Football League clubs.

Curtis began his career at Shelbourne and came over to England to sign for Bristol City in 1956.

After two seasons at Ashton Gate he was transferred to Ipswich Town, and while he was not able to establish a regular first team place in an Ipswich side that boasted of so much talent during the past few years.

He was regarded as a first rate deputy for almost any of the forward positions and continued to hold his place in his country's international side.

Curtis made his debut for Eire in the World Cup qualifying game against Denmark in October 1956, and he has brought his total of appearances to 16, the most recent being against Iceland last August.

Goalkeeper Alan Barnett signed professional for Portsmouth in 1956 after attracting attention with Croydon.

He made a number of First Division appearances for the Fratton Park club before being transferred to Grimsby Town in December 1958.

During his stay with Grimsby his most successful campaign was the season before last when the club won promotion to the Second Division and Barnett played in all but four of the promotion winning games.

John Edgar was introduced to League football by his home town club, Barnsley, and after a number of Second and Third Division games for them moved to Gillingham.

His only season with the Priestfield club saw him successfully top their scoring list with 23 goals in 44 games.

The following term saw him at York City and he was again top scorer, with 15 goals in 42 games. After another season at York, during which injury prevented him from getting many chances, he joined Hartlepool United.

He headed their goalscoring in 1961-62 with 20 goals in 40 appearances, and considering that Hartlepool ended the season next to bottom of the Fourth Division that term, Edgar's contribution was outstanding.

WHO HAS GONE WHERE?
Of the players who left Exeter City at the end of last season, Ray Carter is now with Crawley Town, Mike Hughes (Chesterfield), David Johnston (Stockport County), Jack McMillan (Margate), Charlie Sells (Guildford City), and Colin Tinsley (Luton Town).

Tuesday 3rd September 1963

It was agreed to release Brian Wills from his apprentice professional contract with Exeter City.

Wednesday 4th September 1963

CITY WERE OXFORD SUPERIORS

Football League Cup Round 1
Wednesday 4th September 1963
Manor Ground
Att 5688

Oxford United	0 v 1	Exeter City
Rouse	1	Barnett
Beavon	2	Smyth
Quartermain	3	MacDonald
Atkinson	4	Mitchell
Kyle	5	Harvey
Jones	6	Anderson
Knight	7	Cochrane(1)
Longbottom	8	Henderson
Houghton	9	Curtis
Willey	10	Grace
Harrington	11	Rees

Exeter City sailed into the second round of the Football League Cup for the first time in their history with a display of football which was their best of the season so far.

In every phase of the game, Exeter were Oxford's superiors. The defensive cover was brilliant as Oxford gave up in despair when they were faced with five men on the edge of the penalty area.

The few times that they did get through, they found Alan Barnett in unbeatable form.

City hardly wasted a pass. All through the match the Grecians were a couple of yards faster, and even in the first ten minutes the way they moved the ball drew applause grudgingly from the Oxford crowd.

The all important goal came in the 75th minute. John Cochrane beat Rouse with a fine drive.

After that, City were pushed back on defence, but were totally in command of the

BLANCHFORD & Co., Ltd.
HEADINGTON

on the spot for

FIREPLACES · SINK UNITS · PAINTS · WALLPAPERS
TIMBER & BUILDING MATERIALS

TELEPHONE 63571 (3 lines)

Official Programme — Price Sixpence
Volume 15 ———————— Number 5

FOOTBALL LEAGUE CUP

UNITED
v.
EXETER CITY

WEDNESDAY
4th SEPTEMBER 1963
Kick-off 7.30 p.m.

THE TOP SCORE
TELEVISION REPAIR SERVICE
ANY MAKE - ANY TIME - ANYWHERE

SENIOR RADIO SERVICE LTD.

114 LONDON ROAD, HEADINGTON

WE SUPPLY - WE SERVICE - WE SATISFY

TEL OXFORD
62389

FOR THE SERVICE
THAT HAS SATISFIED
FOR YEARS

situation.

Young Derek Grace was as cool headed and competent as the most experienced man on the field.

He covered a tremendous amount of ground and he fulfilled all the promise that has been shown in the City reserves.

It was a pleasing performance when City won at Bradford on the opening day of the Fourth Division season,, but it was even better against Oxford.

Thursday 5th September 1963

COCHRANE CONSIDERS CITY OFFER
John Cochrane, nearing the completion of a one-month trial with Exeter City, has been offered a full professional contract.

But the Belfast-born winger, who had two seasons with Brighton and Hove Albion before joining the Grecians, has not jumped at the chance.

He still has one week left of his trial and will make a decision at the end of it.

Meanwhile City have released former Bristol City inside-forward Adrian Williams, They have also signed John Symington as a professional, and offered George Ley professional terms as well.

Williams was offered an extension of his trial for another month, but turned it down. Symington, 17, played for Eire at schoolboy and youth international level and looks a useful acquisition. Ley will make a decision to sign professional or not.

Saturday 7th September 1963

CITY LACK CUTTING EDGE

Statistics prove there is a definite pattern to City's play, a pattern which broke down only once at Carlisle, a defensive pattern.

Manager Jack Edwards believes in building his style of football around his players.

At the moment the attack is just not capable of getting a lot of goals. There is a lack of bite and finish among the forwards, partly due to the fact that they have not always had the necessary backing.

They certainly did not have that backing at Gillingham, when the ball came out of defence it found Dermot Curtis on his own with one other man against the combined weight of the Gillingham defence.

Official Programme 6d.

GILLINGHAM FOOTBALL CLUB

SEASON　　　　　　　　1963-64

League Game 4
Saturday 7th September 1963
Priestfield Stadium
Att 8381

Gillingham	0 v 0	Exeter City
Simpson	1	Barnett
Hudson	2	Smyth
Hunt	3	MacDonald
Arnott	4	Mitchell
Burgess	5	Harvey
Farrell	6	Anderson
Ridley	7	Cochrane
Stringfellow	8	Henderson
White	9	Curtis
Gibbs	10	Grace
Pulley	11	Rees

Not surprisingly it was impossible to hold it for long and the rest of the team rarely backed up in time.

Until City get a couple of new forwards or think of another way to get the better backing for the men already there, games will simply follow the same pattern.

It puts a tremendous amount of work on the defence, but there is no doubt so far that it has been extremely successful.

It was successful again at Gillingham and the fact that it was not very inspiring to watch was not the City's fault. They got a point away from home, always a good achievement.

Western League
Exeter City 4 Weymouth 4
Scorers: Exeter City: Riding, Redwood, Ley (2). Weymouth: Cribb (2), Foxley, Mulcairn.
City team: Sidey, Quarrington, Parsons, Northcott, Edmunds, Spiers, Stuckey, Riding, Redwood, Dodd, Ley.
Weymouth team: Clarke, Appleby, Gulliver, Cutting, Newberry, Hall, Tizard, Cribb, Foxley, Mulcairn, Pattie

Wednesday 11th September 1963

FIRST MINUTE WINNER FOR CITY

A slashing cross field ball from George Ley to Graham Rees. A quick pass inside to Arnold Mitchell. A transfer to Dermot Curtis and a shot from the Eire leader and Exeter City had broken Carlisle United with a goal in the first minute of the game.

The goal was a picture, so were the moves that followed and should have brought a bigger score.

Most of the other 89 minutes were good value for money. City moved quickly and slickly, and Carlisle contributed more than their fair share to the game as well.

City were forced to defend for long spells. Carlisle always threatened to score, especially in the last 15 minutes of the game when City's defence took a real

League Game 5
Wednesday 11th September 1963
St James Park
Att 5671

Exeter City	1 v 0	**Carlisle United**
Barnett	1	Dean
Smyth	2	Neil
MacDonald	3	Caldwell
Mitchell	4	Thompson
Harvey	5	Twentyman
Anderson	6	McConnell
Rees	7	Taylor
Henderson	8	McIlmoyle
Curtis(1)	9	Livingstone
Grace	10	Davies
Ley	11	Johnstone

battering.

However, the Grecians hung on for their first home win of the season and stretched their defensive record to four games without conceding a goal.

It was encouraging to see so many chances being created by Exeter. Curtis, John Henderson and Ley all went close with the Carlisle goal having a charmed life at times.

Curtis had his best game yet for City with Derek Grace working like a Trojan. This was a good game to win, for Carlisle are no easy side to beat.

400 UP FOR ARNOLD
Exeter City's long serving player, Arnold Mitchell, reached a significant milestone in the game against Carlisle United at St. James' Park.

Mitchell was making his 400th Football League appearance for the club. He has long since beaten all previous club records for appearances and at his present rate he seems quite likely to go on and create an unassailable record.

He joined Exeter City during the close season of 1952 from Notts County and has played in various positions for the team since then.

The other City players with the most Football League appearances are: Reg Clarke 319 (1927-1939); Keith Harvey 297 (still currently playing); Fred Davey 278 (1947-1956); Charlie Miller (277 (1926-1936).

SULLIVAN WITH HEREFORD UNITED
Former Exeter City defender Derek Sullivan, who left St James' Park for Newport County at the end of the 1961-62, is playing for Hereford United this season. Sullivan, a Welsh International, spent one season at Exeter, having been signed from Cardiff City.

Meanwhile, former City full back Geoff Hudson, who left St James' Park to sign for Crewe Alexandra, is this season playing for Gillingham.

Saturday 14th September 1963

League Game 6
Saturday 14th September 1963
St James Park
Att 5335

DRAB, DULL AND DEPRESSING

Exeter City	1 v 1	Southport
Barnett	1	Rollo
Smyth	2	Cairns
MacDonald	3	Beanland
Mitchell	4	Wallace
Harvey	5	Darvell
Anderson	6	Tighe
Rees	7	Dagger
Henderson	8	Latham
Curtis(1)	9	Blore
Grace	10	Spence
Ley	11	Brookes

Drab, dull and depressing! How can any team play as well in one game as City did against Carlisle United, and then so horribly the next? It is beyond logic.

They played as if they were eight goals up in a practice match instead of fighting for Fourth Division points.

Individually they tried. Collectively they were a failure. They had bits of bad luck, but if they had kept going, then surely they must have scored more than once?

The goal that did come was a good one. Only three men, Alan Barnett, John Henderson and Dermot Curtis touched the ball from the moment it left the City goal mouth, until the Exeter centre-forward hammered it into the net.

That does not excuse the generally shabby display of a forward line who looked as if they had not played together before.

The defence has propped up the rest of the team far too long. This state of affairs cannot last for ever.

City gave away the equalising goal in the 65th minute. A harmless looking cross was allowed to float over the Grecians' defence. The ball struck a post, before Spence rammed in the rebound.

Even so, City are not going to give away too many goals this season, but the question is, are they going to score any? Openings were made, but chances were missed.

WESTERN LEAGUE
Salisbury City 3 Exeter City 1
Scorers: Salisbury City: Pierce, Watts, Palmer. Exeter City: Spiers.
Exeter City team: Parkhill, Quarrington, Parsons, Rutley, Northcott, Edmunds, Rising, Symington, Redwood, Spiers, Stuckey.

THE CHILDREN'S RESEARCH FUND	T. T. JOHNSON
A national charity for the support of research into all children's diseases.	(OPTICIANS) LTD.
Agents and representatives wanted for our football competitions.	Associated with COLLINS AND KITCHISON LTD. PHOTOGRAPHIC & CINE DEALERS
Please write to:-	
THE CHILDREN'S RESEARCH FUND 6, CASTLE STREET, LIVERPOOL 2.	We are specialists in Binoculars and Telescopes 17-19 CATHERINE STREET
	SALISBURY Phone 3123

SALISBURY F.C.

OFFICIAL PROGRAMME

VERSUS

EXETER RES.

SATURDAY
14th SEPT., 1963

3d.

NATIONAL PLAYING FIELDS ASSOCIATION	*PLEASE HELP*
President H.R.H. The Prince Philip, Duke of Edinburgh, K.G., K.T.	**THE DEAF & DEAF-BLIND**
Donations to help in providing playing fields and children's playgrounds throughout the country will be gratefully acknowledged by	*by a GIFT to:*
The General Secretary, 57 Eccleston Square, London, S.W.1	National Institute For The Deaf
	105 Gower Street, London W.C.1

Wednesday 18th September 1963

League Game 7
Wednesday 18th September 1963
Recreation Ground
Att 7063

THAT'S BETTER CITY!

Aldershot	0 v 1	Exeter City
Jones	1	Barnett
Thomas	2	Smyth
Renwick	3	MacDonald
Stepney	4	Mitchell
Henry	5	Harvey
Mulgrew	6	Anderson
Palethorpe	7	Ress
Woan	8	Henderson(1)
Fogg	9	Curtis
Towers	10	Grace
Barton	11	Ley

Exeter City smashed their way onwards and upwards to their best seasons start in five years.

For the few City supporters in the crowd it was a nerve wracking, blood surging 90 minutes, in which the tension or excitement never seemed to lapse.

At first it seemed to be just a case of how long City could hold out as Aldershot bombarded the Exeter goal, but as the game went on, it was Aldershot who ended up struggling.

City gave everything they had for the two points, and they had to, for even in the last minute, Cecil Smyth kicked off the line.

Exeter clicked right back on form. Graham Rees, Dermot Curtis, Arnold Mitchell and Derek Grace went close to scoring in the second half spell when City were stroking the ball from man to man, and the forwards were playing better than at any time this season.

The thing that really put Exeter on top was the 58th minute goal from John Henderson, who slashed the ball into the Aldershot net with a first time shot.

Men of the match were Smyth and Keith Harvey, who completely bottled up the home forwards. Smyth had the greatest game of his two season career, whilst Harvey was so quietly efficient.

Western League
Exeter City 4 Yeovil Town 1
Scorers: Exeter City: Spiers, Stuckey, Symington, Riding. Yeovil Town: Pound.
Exeter City team: Parkhill, Quarrington, Parsons, Rutley, Northcott, Edmunds, Riding, Symington, Redwood, Spiers, Stuckey.

CURTIS IS EXETER CITY'S FIRST EVER INTERNATIONAL
For the first time in the club's history an Exeter City player has been picked to play for his country in a full international.

The player who has brought this honour to the club is centre-forward Dermot Curtis.

He will lead the Eire attack against Austria in Vienna on 25th September. Curtis already has 14 international caps.

A number of Exeter players such as Johnny Nicholls (England) and Derek Sullivan Wales) had represented their countries, but that was before they joined City.

The only other City player to be capped for his country whilst on Exeter's books was P.C. Evans, who was a centre-forward with the club when he played for Wales in 1910, but that was an amateur international.

Two other City players have represented their countries as professionals, but that was not in full internationals, but 'test' matches.

Full-back Stan Charlton, who was a member of the Football Association side which toured Australia in 1925, and inside-left Harold Houghton went to Canada with the F.A. tourists in 1931.

Thursday 19th September 1963

With Exeter City having to travel to Hull City for the second round of the Football League Cup, it will only be the second time that the clubs have met at Boothferry Park.

The other occasion was also in the Cup, but the FA Cup twenty-six years ago, when the Grecians played there in a second round tie and were beaten 2-1.

Goalkeeper Jimmy Parkhill who has been on amateur forms since the start of the season, has now been signed on a full professional contract.

Friday 20th September 1963

DEATH OF BILLY CRAWSHAW
Billy Crawshaw, until 21-years ago, was vice-chairman of Exeter City, has died in a nursing home in Exeter in his late 60s.

He came to Exeter with the Army in 1919 and played a few games as an amateur for City.

On leaving the Forces in the 1920s, he signed professional forms for the club and played right-half for several seasons before leaving to join Accrington Stanley.

Crawshaw was to rejoin Exeter, however, for a second spell at the club, where he ended his playing career.

He became Chairman of the Exeter City Supporters Club and was later appointed to the Board of Directors, becoming vice-chairman. He resigned from the Board in 1961.

Friday 20th September 1963

FOURTH DIVISION TABLE

	P	W	D	L	F	A	Pts
Gillingham	7	3	4	0	6	1	10
Newport County	7	4	2	1	13	6	10
Workington	7	4	2	1	14	9	10
Chesterfield	7	3	3	1	10	8	9
Aldershot	7	4	1	2	17	14	9
Torquay United	7	4	1	2	14	12	9
EXETER CITY	7	3	3	1	5	5	9
Stockport County	7	3	2	2	11	8	8
Halifax Town	7	2	4	1	12	9	8
Darlington	7	2	4	1	10	8	8
Doncaster Rovers	7	3	2	2	13	11	8
Lincoln City	7	3	2	2	8	8	8
Carlisle United	7	3	1	3	17	13	7
Tranmere Rovers	7	3	1	3	14	11	7
Oxford United	7	2	3	2	10	10	7
Barrow	7	2	3	2	9	11	7
Chester	6	2	2	2	8	6	6
Southport	7	1	3	3	10	12	5
Rochdale	6	1	2	3	7	9	4
Bradford City	7	1	2	4	6	10	4
Brighton & H.A.	6	1	1	4	7	10	3
Bradford P.A.	7	1	1	5	8	18	3
Hartlepools United	7	1	1	5	7	22	3
York City	7	0	2	5	6	12	2

Saturday 21st September 1963

LEAGUE DIVISION IV

ALDERSHOT	1	TORQUAY	0
Burton		5294	
BARROW	1	NEWPORT	1
Ackerley		Pring 4370	
BRADFORD CITY	0	HALIFAX TOWN	0
BRIGHTON	1	CHESTERFIELD	1
Goodchild		McQuarrie	7880
CHESTER	1	BRADFORD CITY	0
Corbishley		5569	
EXETER CITY	3	DONCASTER	1
Henderson 2, Curtis		Booth 5775	
GILLINGHAM	2	DARLINGTON	1
Gibbs, Newman		Maltby 8369	
LINCOLN	0	TRANMERE	1
7156		Dyson	
ROCHDALE	5	WORKINGTON	0
Richardson 2, Sturl		3366	
Morton, Kerry			
SOUTHPORT	2	HARTLEPOOLS	1
Spence, Blore		Hinshelwood	3242

GREENSLADES TOURS

Private Party Travel

A Large fleet of Modern Luxury Coaches available for Private Parties

14 QUEEN STREET, EXETER
Telephone 74103

His enthusiasm for sport remained with him all his life and he had been both Captain and President of the Exeter Golf and Country Club.

CITY PLAYERS' BONUS PAYMENTS
With only one defeat in their last eight games, City are hoping for a good attendance for their game against Doncaster Rovers tomorrow.

The players are especially hoping for a good gate, because the City directors have agreed to implement a bonus scheme, whereby players will receive an extra 10/- for a gate of 5,000 and an additional 10/- each for every 500 above that figure.

League Game 8
Saturday 21st September 1963
St James Park
Att 5775

Exeter City	3 v 1	Doncaster Rovers
Barnett	1	Hellewell
Smyth	2	Raine
MacDonald	3	Myers
Mitchell	4	Crompton
Harvey	5	White
Anderson	6	Nibloe
Rees	7	Robinson
Henderson(2)	8	Booth(1)
Curtis(1)	9	Westlake
Grace	10	Hale
Ley	11	Broadbent

Saturday 21st September 1963

CURTIS SHOWS HOW IT IS DONE

Another win for Exeter City, and this time by beating Doncaster Rovers they showed the St James' Park fans the sort of performance which has been getting them the praise and points away from home.

The best thing about it was the way the forward line fell into formation. Dermot Curtis, Graham Rees and John Henderson were always all potential danger men to the Doncaster defence.

There was no doubt though that a tremendous amount of the team's success was due the play of Curtis.

He paved the way for Henderson's 25th minute goal. He also had a hand in the second five minutes later, and then netted the third himself.

With any luck City could have had scored a couple of other goals as they were winners all the way.

It started right from defence and hardly a ball was wasted. The result was that less strain was placed on everyone and the team functioned as a complete unit.

Once again Cecil Smyth was City's outstanding defender and there is no doubt that if he keeps playing as he has done so far this season, then the club will soon be beating off offers for this young Irishman.

Graham Rees also had an impressive game, running rings around Myers, whilst Henderson proved to be a real handful to the Doncaster defence.

Western League
Bath City 2 Exeter City 2
Scorers: Bath City: Owens, Walker. Exeter City: Spiers, Redwood.
Bath City team: Bearpark, Smale, Rideout, Watkins, Swift, Emery, Hobbs, Owens, Stockdale, Barker, Walker.
Exeter City team: Parkhill, Quarrington, Parsons, Rutley, Northcott, Patrick, Riding, Symington, Redwood, Spiers, Stuckey.

Wednesday 25th September 1963

Football League Cup Round 2
Wednesday 25th September 1963
Boothferry Park
Att 9313

Hull City	1 v 0	**Exeter City**
Swan	1	Barnett
Davidson	2	Smyth
Butler	3	MacDonald
Sharpe	4	Mitchell
Milner	5	Harvey
McMillan	6	Anderson
Clarke	7	Rees
Henderson(1)	8	Henderson
Chilton	9	Redwood
Cummins	10	Grace
McSeveney	11	Ley

CITY LACK A CUTTING EDGE

With a bit more experience and power in the forward line, Exeter City could have pulled off a surprise win at Hull City.

In a generally scrappy Football League Cup tie, the game was noted chiefly for missed chances.

Barry Redwood, making his debut, twice almost scored, shooting narrowly wide and straight at Swan. Keith Harvey also went close and City had another effort cleared off the line.

Although Alan Barnett had to pull off three fine saves from Chilton, who also hit the post, Exeter's defence was well marshalled by Arnold Mitchell.

The only time they were beaten was in the 24th minute when Henderson caught them square and flat footed for the only goal of the game.

Although they had less play than Hull, the Grecians were never out of the game and always looked likely to grab an equaliser.

On a number of occasions well planned moves rocked Hull's defence, but generally Exeter were lacking in strength and accuracy needed to finish them off.

Nevertheless City kept Hull supporters on tenterhooks to the final whistle and left the impression that a little more punch in attack, the more important goal of promotion from the Fourth Division should not be beyond them.

Telephone HULL 52001 *(After Hours* HESSLE 61731*)*

NORMAN GILES
—CARS OF QUALITY—

ANY MAKE OF NEW VEHICLE SUPPLIED

H.P. and INSURANCE ARRANGED

EXCHANGES WELCOME

LOW MILEAGE CARS PURCHASED

EXISTING HIRE-PURCHASE SETTLED

96 BOOTHFERRY RD., HULL, YORKS.
(Opposite the Hull City Football Ground)

HULL CITY A.F.C.

BOOTHFERRY PARK · HULL

Official Programme

4D.

v

EXETER CITY

FOOTBALL LEAGUE CUP—2nd ROUND

WEDNESDAY, 25th SEPTEMBER, 1963   Kick-off 7.30 p.m.

SUPPORT YOUR LOCAL INDUSTRY

Ask your repairer for

ManTan SOLE LEATHER

The Leather with the guaranteed wear

THOMAS HOLMES & SONS LIMITED · SCULCOATES · HULL

PARKHILL SIGNS A FULL CONTRACT

Exeter City have signed Irish amateur international goalkeeper, Jimmy Parkhill, as a full professional.

Parkhill who came to the club from Cliftonville in July has been hampered by a groin injury and his original trial period was extended.

There has been some good reports of the few performances he had made in the reserve team, so the keeper was given a full contract.

Western League
Yeovil Town 1 Exeter City 1
Scorers: Yeovil Town: Webber. Exeter City: Spiers.
Exeter City team: Parkhill, Quarrington, Arbury, Rutley, Parsons, Edmunds, Stuckey, Edgar, Riding, Dodd, Spiers.

Saturday 28th September 1963

Football League Game 9
Saturday 28th September 1963
Victoria Ground
Att 2391

Hartlepools United		1 v 1	Exeter City
Oakley		1	Barnett
Wilkie		2	Patrick
Bilcliff		3	MacDonald
Hinchcliffe		4	Mitchell
Atkinson		5	Harvey(1)
Burlison		6	Anderson
McCubbin		7	Smyth
Fraser		8	Henderson
Brown(1)		9	Curtis
Bradley		10	Grace
Lythgo		11	Rees

GRECIANS' USEFUL POINT AT HARTLEPOOL

Exeter City collected another welcome point for their promotion bag at Hartlepool, but it cost them a mighty effort.

City had to fight every inch of the way and they could feel content with the result even though Hartlepool did not get their equaliser until two minutes from time through Brown.

A compact City side had more polish and soccer know how, but it gained little profit from it against the rough and tumble tactics of the home side.

Dermot Curtis was a spirited leader, however, City's attacking hopes rested largely on John Henderson.

The former Charlton Athletic player put in 90 minutes of enthusiastic effort and was only man with a worthwhile shot at his command.

The weakness in attack was that while there was no lack of individual skill, it never matured into a balanced and effective strike force.

THE HARTLEPOOLS UNITED
FOOTBALL & ATHLETIC CLUB CO. LTD.

VICTORIA GROUND . WEST HARTLEPOOL

Photograph by "Northern Daily Mail"

OFFICIAL
PROGRAMME **4**d. 1923
No. 23

Tuesday 1st October

FOURTH DIVISION TABLE

	P	W	D	L	F	A	Pts
Gillingham	9	4	5	0	8	2	13
Newport County	9	4	4	1	15	8	12
Chesterfield	9	4	4	1	12	9	12
EXETER CITY	9	4	4	1	9	7	12
Workington	9	5	2	2	17	15	12
Carlisle United	9	5	1	3	24	14	11
Torquay United	9	5	1	3	18	13	11
Aldershot	9	5	1	3	18	18	11
Stockport County	9	4	2	3	16	10	10
Tranmere Rovers	9	4	2	3	15	11	10
Lincoln City	9	4	2	3	10	9	10
Halifax Town	9	2	5	2	12	11	9
Darlington	9	2	5	2	13	12	10
Chester	8	3	2	3	9	7	8
Southport	9	2	4	3	14	15	8
Barrow	9	2	4	3	10	17	8
Rochdale	8	2	3	3	13	10	7
Brighton & H.A.	9	2	3	4	12	13	7
Oxford United	9	2	3	4	12	15	7
York City	9	2	2	5	11	14	6
Bradford City	9	1	3	5	6	14	5
Hartlepools United	9	1	2	6	9	25	4
Bradford P.A.	9	1	1	7	9	22	3

WESTERN LEAGUE TABLE

	P	W	D	L	F	A	PTS
Welton Rovers	9	7	1	1	23	5	15
Torquay United	10	6	2	2	25	12	14
Bristol City	7	6	1	0	27	6	13
Bridgwater Town	7	6	0	1	12	7	13
Bideford	8	5	1	2	17	8	11
Bath City	9	3	4	2	21	17	10
Yeovil Town	10	3	4	3	18	18	10
Barnstaple Town	7	4	1	2	16	12	9
Weymouth	10	2	5	3	17	20	9
Poole Town	9	3	2	4	18	18	8
EXETER CITY	9	2	3	4	17	17	7
Andover	7	3	1	3	18	19	7
Weston-Super-Mare	8	3	1	4	13	15	7
Salisbury City	8	3	1	4	12	15	7
Chippenham Town	8	3	0	5	11	11	6
Dorchester Town	6	1	4	1	12	12	6
Minehead	7	3	0	4	15	18	6
Bridport	6	1	3	2	7	10	5
Frome Town	7	2	1	4	12	21	5
Glastonbury	8	2	0	6	16	23	4
Portland United	8	1	2	5	15	27	4
Taunton Town	8	1	0	7	1	32	1

For ALL Timber and Building Materials

THE DEVON TRADING COMPANY L^(TD)

EXETER

BRANCHES THROUGHOUT DEVON

Tel: EXETER 71391

Illustrating this was the fact that Keith Harvey got City's 70th minute goal, moving almost up to the goal line to bang home a Graham Rees cross which goalkeeper Oakley could not hold.

In defence as usual, City were solid enough, with Arnold Mitchell, Harvey and Roy Patrick at the top of the credit ratings.

Alan Barnett, despite a buffeting, also did well. Indeed the City keeper twice had to receive treatment for the challenges from the Hartlepool forwards.

WESTERN LEAGUE
Exeter City 0 Weston-Super-Mare 1
Exeter City team: Sidey, Quarrington, Arbury, Rutley, Parsons, Edmunds, Dodd, Edgar, Riding, Spiers, Stuckey.
Weston-Super-Mare team: Robins, Fitzgerald, Chandler, Bass, Owen, Middle, Rivers, Coles, Clare, Norton, Brown.

Tuesday 1st October

CITY BID TURNED DOWN
Exeter City have made a bid for Plymouth Argyle's Adrian Thorne, but their offer was turned down by the Home Park club.

Thorne, a winger or inside forward, has been watched by City for some time and they were keen to bring him to St. James' Park.

At the end of last season he would not re-sign for Plymouth and was transfer listed for a fee of £4,500.

City waited, confident that the Football League would reduce the fee. When they did, the Grecians tried again for the former Brighton and Hove Albion 25-year-old, but they were still told, "no deal."

RECORD START FOR CITY
With Exeter City having sustained only one defeat in the first nine games, a look through the record books reveals that this has not been achieved by the Grecians since the 1919-20 season.

Wednesday 2nd October

CITY LACKED A CUTTING EDGE

Excitement, good football and hard working fast play. All this was packed into the game. In fact, everything but goals.

The City forward line never looked like getting them. Graham Rees positively sparkled

Football League Game 10
Wednesday October 2nd
St James Park
Att 7007

Exeter City	0 v 0	Aldershot
Barnett	1	Jones
Smyth	2	Thomas
MacDonald	3	Renwick
Mitchell	4	Stepney
Harvey	5	Chamberlain
Anderson	6	Mulgrew
Rees	7	Palethorpe
Henderson	8	Kearns
Curtis	9	Fogg
Grace	10	Towers
Ley	11	Burton

on the right wing and almost all the danger came from him, but he had absolutely no support and his excellent work was nearly always wasted.

There was positively no punch in the middle, even allowing for the fact that Aldershot were a good side and that their defence was tightly packed.

City showed they were capable of opening up gaps. They just did not do it often enough. The nearest City came to a goal was when John Henderson shot against a post.

City played some good football, but a lot of this game was defensive for the Grecians.

It was only the effectiveness of an Exeter seven man wall which broke Aldershot down and limited them to just one real shot in the whole game.

Once again Cecil Smyth was the star man in a good, solid defence. City always tried to work the ball out of defence rather than the long clearance up field.

CITY SNIPPETS
City inside forward John Henderson asked the board of directors for permission to combine paying with that of a part time carpenter, however, this was refused.

The Exeter City board of directors were to approach the Football League in order for them to agree to an additional payment to be made to long serving Arnold Mitchell when he made his 400th appearance for the club.

Friday 4th October

CITY ENQUIRE ABOUT IMLACH
Exeter City have made a move to sign former Scottish international winger Stuart Imlach from Crystal Palace. The payer has also appeared for Bury, Derby County, Nottingham Forest, Luton Town and Coventry City. The Lossiemouth-born player has made four appearances for Scotland.

Saturday 5th October 1963

Football League Game 11
Saturday October 5th
St James Park
5965

Exeter City		Darlington
Exeter City	1 v 1	**Darlington**
Barnett	1	Hird
Smyth	2	Whitehead
MacDonald	3	Henderson
Mitchell	4	Potter
Harvey	5	J Robson
Anderson	6	Peverall
Rees	7	Weddle
Henderson	8	Maltby
Curtis(1)	9	Lawton(1)
Grace	10	L Robson
Ley	11	Burbeck

DISAPPOINTING RESULT FOR THE GRECIANS

There were not many satisfied Exeter City fans after this performance. They witnessed Exeter slowly crumble apart against the sort of opposition which they should have beaten by four or five goals.

The team needs strengthening to maintain their position as front runners of the Fourth Division,

In the opening twenty minutes, City rang rings around a shaky Darlington defence. There was little cover in defence and City should have scored at least twice.

The rot gradually set in, spreading back to the normally steady defence. There was very little cover for anyone and certainly no service foe the forwards.

Exeter did stage a late attacking rally and had two shots stopped on the line from Graham Rees and Keith Harvey.

It does not say much for the rest of the forwards when the centre half has to come up and take a pot shot.

There is no excuse for not being able to shoot or find a way through when they are actually on the move.

In the 40th minute Dermot Curtis got the goal from a Arnold Mitchell free-kick which caught the Darlington defence in a state of disarray.

The keeper caught the ball, dropped it as he was challenged by Curtis, who gratefully buried it into the net.

In the second half City's defence began to make mistakes and Darlington equalised with a quick Maltby and Lawton move, the latter scoring, and if they had not been so bad as Exeter, they would have got a couple more.

WESTERN LEAGUE
Bridport 2 Exeter City 2
Scorers: Exeter City: Redwood, Own goal. Bridport: Donovan, Own goal.

EXETER CITY
FOOTBALL CLUB

SATURDAY, OCTOBER 5th, 1963

FOURTH DIVISION

EXETER CITY

versus

DARLINGTON

Kick-off 3.0 p.m.

Official Programme **4ᵈ**

Bridport team: Neal, Darby, Holder, Coulter, Walbridge, White, Whalley, Donovan, Knapman, Skinner, Dailey.
Exeter City team: Parkhill, Quarrington, Patrick, Rutley, Parsons, Spiers, Riding, Symington, Redwood, Edgar, Stuckey.

Monday 7th October 1963

PHOENIX WANTS MORE TIME
Peter Phoenix, the Rochdale left-winger with a goalscoring reputation was due to talk terms with Exeter City today, but in a last minute telephone call he asked for more time to think over the move.

Terms had been agreed between Exeter and Rochdale for this transfer and now everything is up to the player himself.

Born in Manchester, Phoenix joined Oldham Athletic in 1958 and was the leading goalscorer in his first season with them.

After four seasons and more than 150 first team appearances, Phoenix left for Rochdale in 1962 and has been a consistent performer since.

The 26-year-old turned down an offer from Exeter City when he left Manchester City in 1958, preferring to join Oldham and stay in the Manchester area.

Tuesday 8th October 1963

ROCHDALE WINGER SIGNS FOR CITY
Peter Phoenix, the 26-year-old winger from Rochdale signed for Exeter City this afternoon.

After yesterday's hold up City got a shock when Phoenix turned up unannounced at St James' Park today after travelling overnight from Manchester with his wife to talk over conditions of his contract after both clubs had agreed terms.

Exeter City had agreed with Rochdale a fee of £1,400 for the player, £900 of which was to be paid immediately and the remainder on or before 31st December 1963.

CITY MEET HALIFAX FOR FIRST TIME
When Exeter City host Halifax Town at St. James' Park tomorrow evening, it will be the first time that the clubs have met.

Prior to the formation of the Third and Fourth Divisions in 1958, Halifax had spent every one of their League seasons in the Third Division North.

Since the League was reorganised, they have had five seasons in the new Third Division. The clubs have never met in any Cup competition either.

Tuesday 8th October 1963

FOURTH DIVISION TABLE

	P	W	D	L	F	A	Pts
Gillingham	11	6	5	0	13	3	17
EXETER CITY	11	4	6	1	10	8	14
Aldershot	11	6	2	3	22	18	14
Chesterfield	11	5	4	2	13	11	14
Carlisle United	11	6	2	3	32	17	14
Workington	11	6	2	3	21	20	14
Torquay United	11	6	1	4	23	17	13
Stockport County	11	5	2	4	18	12	12
Newport County	11	4	4	3	16	11	12
Lincoln City	11	5	2	4	13	14	12
Chesterfield	10	4	3	3	12	8	11
Tranmere Rovers	11	4	3	4	17	15	11
Brighton & H.A.	11	3	4	4	16	16	10
Halifax Town	11	2	6	3	15	15	10
York City	11	4	2	5	15	15	10
Southport	11	3	4	4	16	17	10
Darlington	11	2	6	3	15	16	10
Doncaster Rovers	11	3	4	4	17	20	10
Rochdale	10	3	3	4	14	12	9
Oxford United	11	3	3	5	15	18	9
Barrow	11	2	5	4	20	21	9
Bradford City	11	2	4	5	10	16	8
Hartlepools United	11	1	3	7	12	34	5
Bradford P.A.	11	1	2	8	12	26	4

WESTERN LEAGUE TABLE

	P	W	D	L	F	A	Pts
Torquay United	11	7	2	2	30	13	16
Welton Rovers	9	7	1	1	23	5	15
Bristol City	8	6	2	0	28	7	14
Bridgwater Town	7	6	0	1	12	7	12
Bath City	10	4	4	2	23	18	12
Bideford	8	5	1	2	17	8	11
Barnstaple Town	8	5	1	2	23	14	11
Yeovil Town	11	3	5	3	19	19	11
Weymouth	11	2	5	4	18	22	9
EXETER CITY	10	2	4	4	19	19	8
Andover	8	3	2	3	20	21	8
Poole Town	10	3	2	5	19	23	8
Chippenham Town	9	3	1	5	13	13	7
Weston-Super-Mare	8	3	1	4	13	15	7
Salisbury City	8	3	1	4	12	15	7
Dorchester Town	6	1	4	1	12	12	6
Minehead	7	3	0	4	15	18	6
Bridport	7	1	4	2	9	12	6
Frome Town	8	2	1	5	14	28	5
Glastonbury	8	2	0	6	16	23	4
Portland United	9	1	2	6	16	31	4
Taunton Town	9	1	1	7	5	33	3

Centre Sea Front
Premier Position
Fully Licensed

Belgrave Hotel, Torquay

Afternoon Teas
Luncheons and Dinners
First Class Accommodation

Football League Game 12
Wednesday October 9th
St James Park
7317

Exeter City	0 v 0	**Halifax Town**
Barnett	1	Downsborough
Smyth	2	Russell
MacDonald	3	Roscoe
Mitchell	4	Jackson
Harvey	5	Richardson
Anderson	6	Harrison
Rees	7	Twist
Phoenix	8	Worthington
Henderson	9	Arnell
Spiers	10	Carlin
Ley	11	Taylor

Wednesday 9th October 1963
SAME OLD STORY IN FRONT OF GOAL

Another draw. That makes five in the first seven home games this season and it is not the way in which Exeter are going to stay at the top end of the Fourth Division.

They had one fault as they fought out a goalless draw with Halifax Town, the old, old fault of not being able to put the ball into the net.

There is no denying that Exeter defended well, fought well and made plenty of openings, but they just could not score. In the end they missed chances because of being over anxious.

There was little fear that Halifax would score and there was always hope that City would score. Exeter did not always look as neat as Halifax, but they were more effective.

Arnold Mitchell, John Henderson, George Spiers, George Ley, Graham Rees and debutant Peter Phoenix all went close to scoring.

It was exasperating not to see City score, but it was heartening to see so many chances being created. What they must do is find extra finishing power.

Phoenix had a competent debut, although out of position. With Dermot Curtis back in the side City may have the answer, but it is one they must find quickly.

It was a far, far better display than last Saturday's draw against Darlington, but City's forwards tended to crowd themselves out when trying to score.

WESTERN LEAGUE
Torquay United 5 Exeter City 2
Scorers: Torquay United: Dart 2, Evans, Rossiter, Own goal. Exeter City scorers: Redwood, Edgar.

Saturday 12th October 1963

Football League Game 13
Saturday October 12th
St James Park
6966

Chester	2 v 0	Exeter City
Reeves	1	Barnett
Molyneux	2	Smyth
J Evans	3	MacDonald
Hauser	4	Mitchell
Butler	5	Harvey
G Evans	6	Anderson
Haddock	7	Rees
Humes	8	Phoenix
Talbot(1)	9	Henderson
Bades	10	Spiers
Lee(1)	11	Ley

DEFEAT NUMBER TWO FOR CITY

Exeter City suffered only their second League defeat of the season at Chester, yet the irritating thing was that at regular intervals throughout this game, City produced patches of near perfect football.

It was as if to prove that they are a superior side and worth their place near the top of the table. Irritating because they never really lived up to those patches of promise.

Nothing really went right for the Grecians. Chester got their goals in the 16th minute from Talbot and in the 50th minute from Lee.

Meanwhile City alternately glided and fumbled around without getting anywhere at times.

The game was lost after the second goal. The idea that City would score three was laughable, for they did not put in one effort that looked like a goal.

Indeed it was not until the closing minutes that Exeter remotely looked like scoring when a header from George Spiers went over the bar.

Alan Barnett was constantly in action in the second half and made saves which verged on the brilliant as Chester strolled around his penalty area taking pot shots.

This was easily City's worst performance of the season and certainly the defence have not played as badly all season.

WESTERN LEAGUE
Taunton Town 0 Exeter City 5
Scorers: Exeter City: Northcott 3, Redwood, Edgar.
Exeter City team: Parkhill, Quarrington, Patrick, Grace, Parsons, Edmunds, Symington, Redwood, Northcott, Edgar, Stuckey.

Monday 14th October 1963

Football League Game 14
Monday October 14th
The Shay
3760

Halifax Town	2 v 0	Exeter City
Downsborough	1	Barnett
Bingley	2	Smyth
Roscoe	3	MacDonald
Jackson(1)	4	Mitchell
Richardson	5	Harvey
Harrison	6	Anderson
Taylor	7	Rees
Bartlett	8	Phoenix
Worthington	9	Henderson
Carlin(1)	10	Spiers
Twist	11	Ley

BLANK WEEKEND FOR CITY

What a poor weekend it has been for Exeter City. No points and no goals from their games at Chester and Halifax.

Whilst the result at Halifax was the same as at Chester two days ago, this time the defence played well, very well in fact.

Apart from what is now accepted as the weakness of the forward line, everything was going to plan for City until well into the second half.

The Grecians, although almost entirely on the defensive, began to move out and it was at this point they could have won the match.

But it was the same old story, creating chances and failing to convert any of them. They certainly had enough shots at goal, but all were comfortably coped with by the Halifax defence.

Having ridden the storm, Halifax began to push City back again and in the 75th minute they scored, when Jackson drove through a crowd of players after Alan Barnett had pushed out a left wing cross.

Three minutes later Carlin got a second with a well placed shot on the run and it was all over for the Grecians as they suffered their worst sequence of results this season.

Wednesday 16th October 1963

CHARLIE VISITS CITY DRESSING ROOM
When Exeter City played Halifax Town on Monday night, they had a visit in the dressing room from an old City player who wished to be remembered to his old team mates and friends at St. James' Park.

Charlie Vowles, who at 73-years-old, was still as fit and as sprightly as ever. The former inside forward joined City after leaving the Services in 1920 and had three seasons with the club alongside players like Dick Pym, Joe Colburne and Jimmy Rigby.

Thursday 17th October 1963

CITY SNIPPET
The Football League notified Exeter City that they had received complaints from other clubs with regards to the standard of the floodlighting at St James' Park. The club informed the Football League that action was being taken to improve the floodlights.

Friday 18th October 1963

ANOTHER ROCHDALE PLAYER TO MOVE TO THE GRECIANS?
Exeter City were hoping to have Rochdale inside forward Ron Cairns in their team tomorrow, but City chairman Reg Rose said today that things have not moved as fast as they had hoped and they are still in the process of negotiation.

City have agreed terms with Rochdale and if Cairns does sign he will team up again with Peter Phoenix who Exeter signed from Dale just over a week ago.

DEREK GRACE WANTS A TRANSFER
Exeter City's promising 18-year-old wing half Derek Grace has asked for a transfer. He was signed two seasons ago from Queen's Park Rangers and has made ten appearances this season.

The reasons for his request are purely personal, as he has to support his mother who lives in London and he cannot do this by earning reserve team money at St. James' Park.

Saturday 19th October 1963

LUCKY CITY

What is keeping Exeter City in the promotion race? Well if this game is anything to go by it is just blind luck, for City deserved to lose by about three goals.

Luck must be backed up with skill and a lot of honest graft, but there was very little of either in this match.

The gamble of playing reserve player, George Northcott, did not come off. Dermot Curtis looked sadly out of touch, so City's attack was no better than before.

City's first goal in four weeks had to come from a defender and it was Cecil Smyth who followed up a piece of quick thinking by running for a throw-in with a 24th minute shot.

Exeter also looked weak at wing half, both Des Anderson and Peter Rutley defended

Friday 18th October 1963

FOURTH DIVISION TABLE

	P	W	D	L	F	A	Pts
Gillingham	14	8	5	1	18	7	21
Carlisle United	14	8	2	4	39	21	18
Workington	14	7	4	3	24	22	18
Aldershot	13	7	3	3	26	20	17
Stockport County	14	5	5	4	21	15	15
Torquay United	14	7	1	6	27	21	15
EXETER CITY	14	4	7	3	10	12	15
Newport County	13	5	4	4	20	16	14
Halifax Town	14	3	8	3	19	17	14
Brighton & H.A.	13	5	4	4	20	18	14
Chesterfield	12	5	4	3	14	14	14
Lincoln City	13	6	2	5	16	17	14
Doncaster Rovers	14	5	4	5	23	23	14
Chester	12	5	3	4	14	9	13
Tranmere Rovers	13	4	4	5	20	19	12
Southport	14	4	4	6	18	21	12
Darlington	13	3	6	4	17	19	12
Barrow	14	3	5	6	17	27	11
Rochdale	11	3	4	4	15	13	10
York City	13	4	2	7	17	19	10
Oxford United	13	3	4	6	19	25	10
Bradford City	13	3	4	6	19	25	10
Hartlepools United	13	3	3	7	16	36	9
Bradford P.A.	13	2	2	9	18	31	6

WESTERN LEAGUE

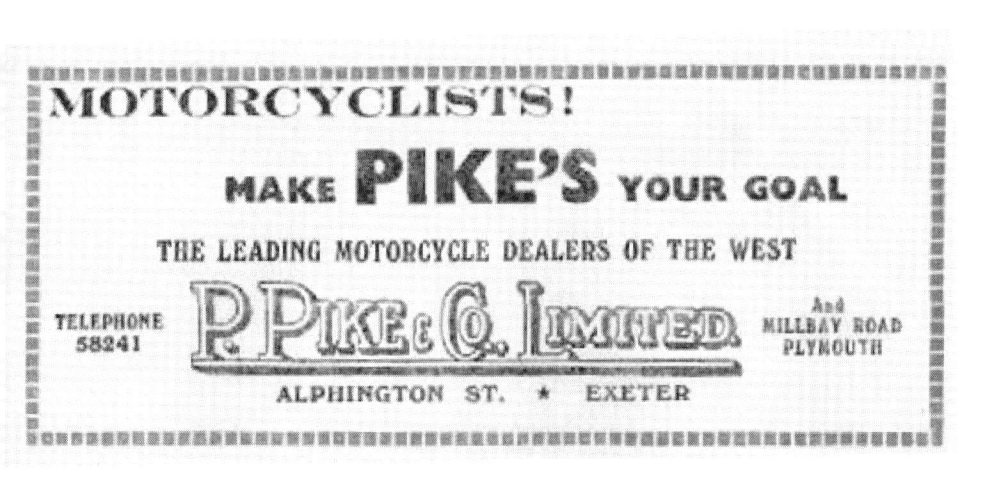

	P	W	D	L	F	A	Pts
Torquay United	13	8	2	3	35	16	18
Bristol City	9	7	2	0	31	8	16
Welton Rovers	11	7	1	3	25	13	15
Bridgwater Town	8	7	0	1	16	8	14
Bideford	9	6	1	2	22	9	13
Barnstaple Town	9	6	1	2	27	17	13
Yeovil Town	12	4	5	3	20	19	13
Bath City	11	4	4	3	25	21	12
EXETER CITY	12	3	4	5	26	24	10
Weymouth	12	2	6	4	19	23	10
Andover	9	3	3	3	21	22	9
Salisbury City	9	4	1	4	15	17	9
Weston-Super-Mare	9	3	2	4	14	16	8
Poole Town	11	3	2	6	20	27	8
Dorchester Town	7	1	5	1	13	13	7
Chippenham Town	10	3	1	6	16	17	7
Glastonbury	9	3	0	6	21	25	6
Minehead	9	3	0	4	15	18	6
Bridport	8	1	4	3	11	17	6
Portland United	10	2	2	6	20	34	6
Frome Town	9	2	1	6	17	32	5
Taunton Town	10	1	1	8	5	38	3

MOTORCYCLISTS!
MAKE PIKE'S YOUR GOAL
THE LEADING MOTORCYCLE DEALERS OF THE WEST

TELEPHONE 58241

P. Pike & Co. Limited

And MILLBAY ROAD PLYMOUTH

ALPHINGTON ST. ★ EXETER

Football League Game 15
Saturday October 19th
St James Park
5549

Exeter City	1 v 0	York City
Barnett	1	Forgan
Smyth (1)	2	Baker
MacDonald	3	Geron
Rutley	4	Woods
Harvey	5	Jackson
Anderson	6	Ashworth
Rees	7	Gould
Curtis	8	Wiliinson
Northcott	9	Meechan
Edgar	10	Rudd
Phoenix	11	Lang

competently, but as midfield inks or added power to the forward line they were non existent.

Only John Edgar, returning after a long lay off with knee trouble, impressed in the forward line. Although he did not seem fully fit there is no doubt that no one else can match his distribution of the ball.

WESTERN LEAGUE
Glastonbury 4 Exeter City 4
Scorers: Glastonbury: Hawkins, Allen, Llewellyn, Vowells. Exeter City: Redwood, Ley, Stuckey, Riding.
Glastonbury team: Rew, Williams, Clark, O'Donnell, Vowells, Hawkins, Allen, Llewellyn, Fox, Edmonds, Walton.
Exeter City team: Parkhill, Quarrington, Arbury, Henderson, Parsons, Grace, Stuckey, Riding, Redwood, Symington, Ley.

CITY SNIPPETS
Former Exeter City defender Alvan Williams is now trainer/coach at Hartlepools United. Williams joined the Grecians from Bradford Park Avenue in 1960 and went on to score one goal in nineteen league appearances.

Wednesday 23rd October 1963

AT LAST: CITY FIND THE NET!

Everything that has gone wrong with Exeter City's much maligned and moaned about forward line went right against Tranmere Rovers.

City clicked at last. They fought all the way and dictated the game throughout.

Football League Game 16
Wednesday October 23rd
St James Park
5701

Exeter City	5 v 0	Tranmere Rovers
Barnett	1	Leyland
Smyth	2	Wilson
MacDonald	3	Oxtoby
Mitchell(1)	4	King
Harvey	5	Manning
Anderson	6	Gubbins
Rees(1)	7	Campbell
Edgar	8	Jones
Curtis(1)	9	Evans
Henderson(1)	10	Dyson
Phoenix(1)	11	Roberts

No one fought harder than Arnold Mitchell, back like a brand new man after a one game rest. He seemed to be everywhere in defence and prompting the forwards.

City opened the scoring in the 14th minute. Les MacDonald's free kick was chested toward goal by Dermot Curtis, Leyland pushed the ball out, but Peter Phoenix cracked in a great shot.

Four minutes later Mitchell scored from a Graham Rees corner with a crashing shot.

In the 51st minute Curtis finished off a John Henderson and John Edgar move. After that it was a question of how many City would score.

It was a long wait though, for it wasn't until the 84th minute that Exeter found the net again, Rees scoring with a shot from Edgar's low cross.

A minute from time it was 5-0 as Henderson swept the ball into the net for City's biggest win since April 1962.

The forwards at last showed they can attack constructively and take chances. The whole team showed that they can fight with determination.

Friday 25th October 1963

GRECIANS PART WITH THEIR RECORD FEE
Exeter City made two signings today and had to pay a club record fee for one of them. He was Alan Banks, 25, an inside forward from Cambridge City.

City have to pay two separate transfer fees for the player, one to Southern League club Cambridge City and one to his former club, Liverpool.

The Grecians paid Cambridge City £3,000, plus a further £250 after Banks had played twenty first team appearances. £2,000 of which would be paid immediately with the remainder on or before 25th December 1963.

In addition City paid £2,000 to Liverpool, £1,000 of which was paid immediately, the balance to be forwarded by 31st December 1963.

City chairman Reg Rose said his transfer fee includes one of the biggest fees that the club has had to pay, but it should be well worth it with his goal scoring record.

Banks certainly has an outstanding scoring record. During his two and a half season stay with Cambridge City, he has scored a total of 120 goals.

Last season he scored 48 goals in 35 matches, despite a knee injury that kept him out of action. At one period last season Banks scored goals in 25 consecutive games.

Originally with Liverpool for four years, one of them as an amateur, during that time Banks scored seven goals in eight first team appearances.

City director Les Kerslake has been with Banks for the past two days, fighting strong competition from other League clubs who wanted to sign him.

This morning Banks agreed terms to sign for Exeter City and said that he had chosen the Grecians because he likes this part of the world very much and the club offered him first class accommodation.

The other signing City have made today is that of 24-year-old half back Ray Gough from Linfield.

He is an Irish youth international and has played two games for the League of Ireland side. Exeter have, had to pay a fee of £150 for him.

They have also agreed that should the player want to return to Ireland that he be transferred back to Linfield.

Gough was recommended to City by Jackie Milburn, now manager of Ipswich Town, and formerly of Linfield.

Whilst at Linfield, Gough featured in three Irish League Cup Finals, and was on the winning side in two of them.

Saturday 26th October 1963

A GAME OF TWO PENALTIES

They started badly and got worse, that was Exeter City at Barrow. City allowed themselves to be dragged down to their lowest level of the season and yet they got a point, when Keith Harvey scored from the penalty spot in injury time after a John Henderson shot had been handled.

Everything that went right against Tranmere Rovers in the previous match went wrong again this time around. The defence was worse than the forward line for once.

The game started scruffily and it stayed that way. Barrow had less skill even than City,

Football League Game 17
Saturday October 26th
Holker Street
3214

Barrow	1 v 1	Exeter City
Caine	1	Barnett
Arrowsmith	2	Smyth
Cahill	3	MacDonald
Hale	4	Mitchell
O'Neill	5	Harvey(1)
Clark	6	Anderson
Maddison	7	Rees
Darwin	8	Edgar
Ackerley	9	Curtis
Thompson	10	Henderson
Kemp	11	Phoenix

but they made less mistakes and so had more of the play.

It is true City were not helped by an injury to Dermot Curtis which sent him playing out the game on the wing, but no side should allow themselves to become as disorganised as they were.

Alan Barnett saved a first minute penalty from Darwin and everything else that came his way except for Kemp's second half goal was easily dealt with.

In spite of all the criticism it is a change to see City getting some luck and the run of the ball when they play badly, but they cannot rely on getting away with it like this for long.

WESTERN LEAGUE
Exeter City 1 Poole Town 2
Scorers: Exeter City: Riding. Poole Town: Saker 2.
Exeter City team: Parkhill, Quarrington, Patrick, Grace, Parsons, Edmunds, Stuckey, Riding, Redwood, Symington, Ley.
Poole Town team: Chandler, Penzer, Stark, Hesse, Brown, Wembridge, Bodger, Male, Saker, McDowell, Brewster.

Monday 28th October 1963

BANKS IS AN IMMEDIATE SUCCESS

Alan Banks is a big success, full of fight and fire. He could have scored three times in the first half and it was only brilliant saves by Leyland that prevented him from doing so.

In the whole 90 minutes he never gave up as his new team mates plied him with passes. He figured in almost every attack.

In the 75th minute Banks rounded the keeper but his shot was fisted out by Oxtoby. Keith Harvey scored with his second successive penalty kick.

Unfortunately for Banks and Exeter City, they still came away from Tranmere a

Football League Game 18
Monday October 28th
Prenton Park
5471

Tranmere Rovers	2 v 1	Exeter City
Leyland	1	Barnett
Wilson	2	Smyth
Conroy	3	MacDonald
King	4	Mitchell
Oxtoby	5	Harvey(1)
Gubbins	6	Anderson
Campbell	7	Rees
McDonnell	8	Banks
Evans	9	Henderson
Dyson(1)	10	Edgar
Roberts(1)	11	Phoenix

beaten side, but it was a performance that was a 100% improvement from the whole team.

The defence had a bit of a shaky start and gave away an early goal after ten minutes when Roberts ran in to beat Barnett with an angled shot.

Tranmere's second goal came from a Dyson snap shot in the 65th minute which went in off the underside of the crossbar.

Harvey's penalty reduced the arrears and City went all out for that equaliser, but did not quite do it.

There was no disgrace in this defeat. The Grecians got more praise for this than the scrambled point at Barrow.

CARTILAGE OPERATION FOR WELSH
Exeter City right winger Eric Welsh entered hospital today for a cartilage operation. The Irish winger has been out of action since the start of the season.

Tuesday 29th October 1963

CITY SNIPPETS
Exeter City's former Southampton full back, Roy Patrick asked the club for a transfer.

Saturday 2nd November 1963

GRECIANS LOSE UNBEATEN HOME RECORD

This performance is hardly likely to inspire the City spectators. It was not that Exeter lost their home record, but it was the way that they lost it.

Rochdale played a simple, deep lying centre forward formation and lost the City completely. They had all the time in the world to work the ball and had Exeter running all ways.

Rochdale took a 14th minute lead after a three man move split the City defence and ended with Richardson scoring.

Friday 1st November 1963

FOURTH DIVISION TABLE

	P	W	D	L	F	A	Pts
Gillingham	18	10	5	3	21	8	25
Carlisle United	18	10	4	4	47	22	24
Workington	17	9	5	3	31	25	23
Brighton & H.A.	18	7	5	6	28	20	20
EXETER CITY	18	6	8	4	18	15	20
Torquay United	18	9	2	7	33	26	20
Chester	17	7	5	5	17	10	19
Oxford United	18	7	5	6	30	27	19
Chesterfield	15	7	4	4	21	18	18
Stockport County	18	5	8	5	21	15	18
Aldershot	18	7	4	7	31	33	18
Bradford City	18	7	4	7	27	27	18
Newport County	17	6	5	6	28	28	17
Doncaster Rovers	18	6	5	7	29	30	17
Darlington	17	5	7	5	21	26	17
Lincoln City	18	7	3	8	23	31	17
Halifax Town	18	4	8	6	22	28	16
York City	18	6	3	9	24	25	15
Tranmere Rovers	17	5	4	8	25	32	14
Southport	18	5	4	9	23	32	14
Rochdale	16	4	6	6	21	19	14
Barrow	16	3	7	6	18	28	13
Hartlepools United	16	3	5	8	16	38	11
Bradford P.A.	18	3	5	10	25	36	11

WESTERN LEAGUE TABLE

	P	W	D	L	F	A	Pts
Torquay United	15	9	2	4	39	19	20
Bristol City	10	8	2	0	34	9	18
Welton Rovers	13	8	1	4	27	16	17
Bridgwater Town	9	8	0	1	19	8	16
Yeovil Town	13	5	5	3	24	20	15
Bideford	10	6	2	2	23	10	14
Barnstaple Town	11	6	2	3	29	22	14
Salisbury City	11	6	1	4	18	17	13
Weymouth	14	3	7	4	25	24	13
Bath City	12	4	4	4	26	25	12
Chippenham Town	12	5	1	6	22	18	11
EXETER CITY	14	3	5	6	31	30	11
Andover	11	4	3	4	24	24	11
Minehead	9	5	0	4	19	19	10
Poole Town	14	4	2	8	23	31	10
Weston-Super-Mare	11	3	3	5	16	20	9
Dorchester Town	8	1	6	1	14	14	8
Portland United	12	3	2	7	21	36	8
Glastonbury	11	3	1	7	26	33	7
Frome Town	11	3	1	7	22	35	7
Bridport	11	1	4	6	13	30	6
Taunton Town	12	1	2	9	6	41	4

HOLMAN HAM & Co., Ltd.

Family Chemists

EXETER

SOUTH STREET FORE STREET, HEAVITREE
ST. ANN'S PHARMACY, SIDWELL STREET
POLSLOE BRIDGE COWICK STREET
GLASSHOUSE LANE, COUNTESS WEIR
BIRCHY BARTON HILL BEACON LANE

Also Branches in Devon, Somerset and Dorset

TRANMERE ROVERS
Football Club Ltd.

UBI FIDES IBI LUX ET ROBUR

ROVERS v. EXETER CITY

Monday, October 28th, 1963.
Official Programme 3d.

YATES
BITTER BEER
FOR TOP QUALITY

Printed by E. Shaw & Co. Ltd., Church Road, Wallasey.

Football League Game 19
Saturday November 2nd
St James Park
6249

Exeter City	0 - 1	Rochdale
Barnett	1	Burgin
Smyth	2	Wells
Patrick	3	Winton
Mitchell	4	Hepton
Harvey	5	Milburn
Anderson	6	Thompson
Rees	7	Cairns
Banks	8	Richardson(1)
Curtis	9	Watson
Henderson	10	Morton
Phoenix	11	Storf

In the second half City made a few reshuffles which seemed to only make matters worse.

It was only in the last 15 minutes that the Grecians seemed to realise that to salvage anything from the game they had to attack, and when they did, it was too late.

Burgin made two good saves from Dermot Curtis and Peter Phoenix, but then Rochdale were unfortunate to have a shot stopped on the line by Roy Patrick and another headed over by Cecil Smyth.

The only way that City could make an accurate pass was backwards, and because of their lack of control, their other attacks were a series of solo dashes.

Alan Banks always looked potentially the most dangerous man in the side and he was certainly a consistent fighter.

He was on his own most of the time and when he did make a chance there was no one else to take it.

WESTERN LEAGUE
Weston-Super-Mare 0 Exeter City 2
Scorers: Exeter City: Northcott, Spiers.
Exeter City team: Parkhill, Quarrington, MacDonald, Rutley, Northcott, Gough, Stuckey, Symington, Redwood, Edgar, Spiers.

WILL ALAN BANKS BE THE ANSWER?
Football club directors area much maligned group of sportsmen. Everyone it seems is ready to criticise them and they seldom get much praise or thanks from their club supporters.

Therefore the Exeter City board of directors should be praised for their recent all out efforts to obtain the players needed to strengthen the teams' forward line and keep the Grecians in the promotion race.

After the signing of Alan Banks, no one can complain that City are not doing everything in their power to make this our promotion year.

We will have to wait and see whether Alan Banks fits into the City's scheme of things, but according to his record he is one of the finest captures made by the Grecians since the war.

Only last week the national magazine 'Soccer Star' had this to say:-

'Alan Banks, the Cambridge City goalscoring 'machine' wants to move from the East Anglian club. He is still on Liverpool's list at £5,000 and any move to a Football League club would mean a larger fee than that.'

In an earlier issue of the same magazine, we have read the following:-

'Banks was (last season) without doubt the outstanding player in the Southern League. His goalscoring ability was little short of phenomenal.'

Thursday 7th November 1963

CITY SNIPPET
Exeter City inside forward John Henderson was interesting Chesterfield who made an enquiry about the player.

Friday 8th November 1963

CITY BOSS WARNED BY F.A.
Exeter City manager Jack Edwards has been severely censured by the Football Association disciplinary committee after a report by the referee in charge of the Exeter versus Darlington match played on 5th October.

Edwards was warned as to his future conduct and ordered to give a written undertaking to the Football Association not to repeat his misconduct for which he had been reported.

MacDONALD SIGNS NEW CONTRACT
Exeter City left back Les MacDonald who has been on a series of monthly contracts since the start of the season has now agreed to re-sign for the rest of the season. He has also asked to be removed from the club's transfer list.

Saturday 9th November 1963

MITCHELL INSPIRES CITY TO VICTORY

For the second time this season Exeter City have won at Oxford United's Manor Ground. The team played with a plan and purpose.

The football started from the back and moved sweetly, and smoothly, though the entire team and the end product was two goals.

Arnold Mitchell was the star, spraying out passes from every point of the pitch. An invaluable link man, Derek Grace, who was playing alongside Mitchell, showed great

BLANCHFORD & CO., LTD.
HEADINGTON
on the spot for
FIREPLACES · SINK UNITS · PAINTS · WALLPAPERS
TIMBER & BUILDING MATERIALS
TELEPHONE 63571 (3 lines)

Official Programme — Price Sixpence
Volume 15 ——————— Number 13

FOOTBALL LEAGUE
(FOURTH DIVISION)

UNITED

v.

EXETER

SATURDAY
9th NOVEMBER 1963
Kick-off 3 p.m.

THE TOP SCORE
TELEVISION REPAIR SERVICE
ANY MAKE   -   ANY TIME   -   ANYWHERE
SENIOR RADIO SERVICE
LTD.
114 LONDON ROAD. HEADINGTON
WE SUPPLY   -   WE SERVICE   -   WE SATISFY

TEL
OXFORD
62389
FOR THE SERVICE
THAT HAS SATISFIED
FOR YEARS

Football League Game 20
Saturday November 9th
Manor Ground
7185

Oxford United	0 v 2	Exeter City
Fearnley	1	Barnett
Cassidy	2	Smyth
Quartermain	3	MacDonald
Atkinson	4	Mitchell
Kyle	5	Harvey
Jones	6	Anderson
Knight	7	Rees
Longbottom	8	Banks(1)
Cornwell	9	Curtis(1)
Willey	10	Grace
Harrington	11	Phoenix

confidence and style.

Of course it was not all sweetness and light for the City. There were times when they struggled and there were times when they made mistakes, but there were never the shambles of the last few weeks.

Once Dermot Curtis put in a long shot in the 30th minute that dropped in over the head of Fearnley, it seemed certain they had the game sewn up.

After 15 minutes of the second half it was a certainty as everyone blotted out the best that Oxford could produce and generally they started to move forward.

Alan Banks scored his first goal for Exeter with a great flying header in the 63rd minute and Mitchell, Graham Rees, Grace and Curtis could easily have scored others.

Such was the grip that City had on this game that they strolled around flicking the ball from man to man for minutes on end.

WESTERN LEAGUE
Exeter City 0 Barnstaple Town 3
Scorers: Barnstaple Town: Marshall 2, Langman.
Exeter City team: May, Quarrington, Parsons, Rutley, Northcott, Gough, Stuckey, Spiers, Redwood, Symington, Ley.
Barnstaple Town team: Berry, Gray, Penford, Meadows, Hancock, Chapman, Marshall, Pulman, Langman, Fewings, Arundel.

HARROWER AT ST. MARKS
Former Exeter City, Torquay United and Third Lanark inside forward Bill Harrower, who is now 41-years-old, is this season playing for St. Marks in the Exeter and District League.

Harrower signed for the Grecians from Torquay in July 1948 and went on to net 11 goals in 85 league appearances.

Thursday 14th November 1963

CITY SNIPPET
It was announced that the Exeter City team and manager were to have a pre-match lunch at The Imperial Hotel, Exeter, prior to their FA Cup tie against Shrewsbury Town at St James' Park.

Friday 15th November 1963

FOURTH DIVISION TABLE

	P	W	D	L	F	A	Pts
Gillingham	20	12	5	3	25	9	29
Carlisle United	20	11	5	4	49	24	27
Workington	19	10	6	3	34	26	26
Torquay United	20	10	3	7	43	29	23
Brighton & H.A.	20	8	6	6	32	24	22
EXETER CITY	20	7	8	5	20	16	22
Chester	19	8	5	6	22	13	21
Bradford City	20	8	4	8	30	31	20
Aldershot	20	8	4	8	36	41	20
Darlington	19	6	8	5	24	28	20
Lincoln City	20	8	4	8	26	35	20
Stockport County	20	5	9	6	22	21	19
Chesterfield	18	7	6	5	22	20	19
Halifax Town	20	5	9	6	35	34	19
Newport County	19	7	5	7	32	32	19
Oxford United	20	7	5	8	31	31	19
Rochdale	18	6	6	6	26	19	18
Doncaster Rovers	20	6	6	8	30	35	18
York City	20	6	4	10	24	26	16
Tranmere Rovers	19	5	5	9	28	36	15
Southport	20	5	5	10	26	39	15
Barrow	18	3	8	7	21	34	14
Hartlepools United	18	4	5	9	18	41	13
Bradford P.A.	20	3	6	11	31	46	12

WESTERN LEAGUE

	P	W	D	L	F	A	Pts
Torquay United	17	9	3	5	41	22	21
Bristol City	12	8	4	0	35	10	20
Welton Rovers	14	9	2	4	31	18	20
Bideford	12	8	2	2	30	10	18
Bridgwater Town	11	9	0	2	21	10	18
Barnstaple Town	13	7	2	4	33	24	16
Yeovil Town	15	5	6	4	27	25	16
Chippenham Town	14	7	1	6	26	19	15
Salisbury City	13	7	1	5	21	19	15
Andover	13	5	4	4	31	29	14
Weymouth	15	3	8	4	27	26	14
EXETER CITY	16	4	5	7	33	33	13
Bath City	14	4	5	5	31	32	13
Minehead	10	6	0	4	23	20	12
Dorchester Town	10	2	7	1	18	15	11
Glastonbury	13	5	1	7	31	35	11
Frome Town	13	4	2	7	27	38	10
Poole Town	16	4	2	10	24	36	10
Weston-Super-Mare	13	3	3	7	17	26	9
Portland United	14	3	3	8	23	41	9
Bridport	13	1	4	8	13	37	6
Taunton Town	14	1	3	10	7	45	5

Saturday 16 November 1963

FA CUP ROUND ONE

First Round proper day of the FA Cup brought the usual mix of shocks and drama.

The biggest upset came at The Huish where Yeovil Town defeated Southend United of the Third Division by one goal to nil. Non-League teams gaining creditable draws included Kettering Town (at home to Millwall), Margate (Away to Brentford) and Enfield (away to Reading).

Gateshead, who had left the Football League a few years earlier, were 4-1 winners at Darlington.

Two matches were postponed due to heavy fog affecting the North West of the country. The match at Altrincham was abandoned with just 12 minutes left to play as the fog descended on Moss Lane.

16/11/63	Altrincham	Wrexham	1-2	9000 ABD Fog
16/11/63	Barnsley	Stockport County	1-0	7577
16/11/63	Barrow	Bangor City	3-2	4787
16/11/63	Bexley United	Wimbledon	1-5	4968
16/11/63	Bournemouth	Bristol Rovers	1-3	12402
16/11/63	Bradford (PA)	Heanor Town	3-1	5799
16/11/63	Bradford City	Port Vale	1-2	8147
16/11/63	Brentford	Margate	2-2	12150
16/11/63	Bridgwater Town	Luton Town	0-3	5000
16/11/63	Brighton	Colchester	0-1	14419
16/11/63	Cambridge United	Chelsford City	0-1	7536
16/11/63	Chester	Blyth Spartans	3-2	9366
16/11/63	Corby Town	Bristol City	1-3	4920
16/11/63	Crook Town	Chesterfield	1-2	3234
16/11/63	Crystal Palace	Harwich & Parkeston	8-2	15759
16/11/63	Darlington	Gateshead	1-4	6135
16/11/63	Doncaster Rovers	Tranmere Rovers	3-0	5622
16/11/63	Exeter City	Shrewsbury Town	2-1	7232
16/11/63	Hartlepools United	Lincoln City	0-1	5698
16/11/63	Hereford United	Newport County	1-1	7000
16/11/63	Hull City	Crewe Alexandra	2-2	10013
16/11/63	Kettering Town	Millwall	1-1	5000
16/11/63	Maidenhead United	Bath City	0-2	4628
16/11/63	Netherfield	Loughborough United	6-1	2000
16/11/64	Notts County	Frickley Colliery	2-1	5896
16/11/65	Oldham Athletic	Mansfield Town	PPD	
16/11/66	Oxford United	Folestone	2-0	7294
16/11/67	Peterborough United	Watford	1-1	15163
16/11/68	QPR	Gillingham	4-1	12141
16/11/69	Reading	Enfield	2-2	10178
16/11/70	Rochdale	Chorley	PPD	
16/11/71	Southport	Walsall	2-1	4768
16/11/63	Sutton United	Aldershot	0-4	6213
16/11/63	Tooting & Mitcham	Gravesend & Northfleet	1-2	5000
16/11/63	Torquay United	Barnet	6-2	6394
16/11/63	Trowbridge Town	Coventry City	1-6	6524
16/11/63	Weymouth	Bedford	1-1	5000
16/11/63	Workington	Halifax Town	4-1	5967
16/11/63	Yeovil Town	Southend United	1-0	7631
16/11/63	York City	Carlisle United	2-5	7342

Exeter City's home game against Stockport County has been brought forward a day from Saturday afternoon to the Friday evening, so as not to clash with the visit of the All Blacks to Exeter where they will meet a South West Counties team at the County Ground.

F.A. CUP TIME AGAIN
It is FA Cup time again this Saturday and this most exciting of all football competitions always gets the fans on tip-toe and sees Exeter City eager as ever for a long run that will stimulate local interest in the club.

City have not enjoyed a great deal of success in the FA Cup since 1950-51 when they went through to the fourth round and held First Division Chelsea to a 1-1 draw at St James' Park, before losing the replay 2-0 at Stamford Bridge.

Indeed it is now eight years since Exeter City last defeated a Football League club in the first round of the competition.

After three consecutive first round defeats against Bournemouth, Dartford and Gravesend respectively, the Grecians are keener than ever to progress against Saturday's visitors to the Park, Shrewsbury Town.

It is five years since Exeter City last met Shrewsbury Town, and they just beat City by one point to win promotion from the Fourth Division in 1958-59, the first season of this new Division.

It is unfortunate that new signing Alan Banks is cup-tied, having already played for Cambridge City in this season's FA Cup.

Saturday 16th November 1963

ANDERSON IS THE UNLIKELY MATCH WINNER

This performance was one to be proud of, for any side to find themselves a goal down in the first minute an fight back to win must have played well.

There could not have been a more dramatic start than Shrewsbury's goal in thirty seconds from Middleton's well placed shot.

It was a start that was designed to shatter City and it almost did as they struggled to find their feet in a bewildering opening ten minutes.

After two narrow misses, Dermot Curtis made it third time lucky as he slid a headed ball from George Northcott over the line.

Gradually City came to grips with the Third Division side. The winning goal came in

FA Cup Round 1
Saturday November 16th
St James Park
7232

Exeter City	2 v 1	Shrewsbury Town
Barnett	1	Boswell
Smyth	2	Wright
MacDonald	3	Turner
Mitchell	4	Harley
Harvey	5	Dolby
Anderson(1)	6	Hemsley
Rees	7	Gregson
Northcott	8	Ross
Curtis(1)	9	Clarke
Grace	10	Brodie
Phoenix	11	Middleton(1)

the 72nd minute from Des Anderson, who had never scored before in his career. A Cup dream come true.

With Alan Banks cup-tied, Northcott was recalled to the team and although he did not have the speed and dash, he had what was needed on the day, the ability to continually upset the Shrewsbury defence and touches that helped bring both goals.

The chances of meeting a side as good as Shrewsbury in the second round must be slim and if City play like this, there is no reason why they could not make it to the third round.

WESTERN LEAGUE
Portland United 4 Exeter City 3
Scorers: Portland United: Harve 2, Tizard, Robinson. Exeter City: Rutley, Stuckey, Redwood.
Exeter City team: Parkhill, Quarrington, Parsons, Rutley, Gough, Edmunds, Stuckey, Riding, Redwood, Symington, Ley.

Thursday 21st November 1963

F.A. CUP TIE: ALL TICKET
Exeter City's second round F.A. Cup tie against Bristol City on 7th December will be an all ticket game.

This is the first all ticket match at St James' Park since October 1960 when Manchester United were the visitors in the Football League Cup.

It has been announced that admission prices are not being increased, and they will therefore be as for a normal League game.

Saturday 23rd November 1963

A SLOG IN THE MUD

A large contingent of Exeter City supporters were at Somerton Park to see Exeter City defeat Newport County by the only goal of the game.

Football League Game 21
Saturday November 23rd
Somerton Park
3339

Newport County	0 v 1	Exeter City
Weare	1	Barnett
Bird	2	Smyth
Walters	3	MacDonald
Williams	4	Mitchell
Rathbone	5	Harvey
Rowland	6	Anderson
Kear	7	Rees
Webster	8	Banks(1)
Bonson	9	Curtis
Hunt	10	Grace
Smith	11	Phoenix

It was hard going fighting the Welsh side and the mud at the same time. It was a calculated slog rather than a flash of inspiration that got this win.

Right from the start the whole team settled down to successfully smother the Newport raiders, then click into their own attacking combination.

The game never really settled down to any pattern except for a series of savagely chopping and hacking attacks at either end.

City were far more organised and accurate in midfield and it was only this which made them worth their win.

Alan Banks was the man who grabbed the goal as he ran onto a Cecil Smyth cross to head past Weare just four minutes from the end.

Behind Banks the defence kept a record which speaks for itself. It was the fourth best defensive record in the Football League.

City are now fifth in the Fourth Division table and people are beginning to talk about the club again throughout Exeter and the possibility of promotion.

Supporters are travelling to away games again and at last Exeter City are coming alive after four seasons of failure and frustration.

WESTERN LEAGUE
Exeter City 1 Welton Rovers 3
Scorers: Exeter City: Ley. Welton Rovers: Barker 2, Chedgy.
Exeter City team: Parkhill,. Quarrington, Arbury, Rutley, Parsons, Gough, Stuckey, Redwood, Riding, Spiers, Ley.
Welton Rovers team: Norman, Campbell, Millard, Slocombe, Hendy, Chedgy, Painter, Comer, Barker, Allen, Boxley.

Thursday 28th November 1963

FOURTH DIVISION TABLE

	P	W	D	L	F	A	Pts
Gillingham	21	12	5	4	26	12	29
Workington	20	11	6	3	36	27	28
Carlisle United	21	11	5	5	51	27	27
Brighton & H.A.	21	9	6	6	37	24	24
EXETER CITY	21	8	8	5	21	16	24
Chester	20	9	5	6	26	15	23
Torquay United	21	10	3	8	43	32	23
Aldershot	21	9	4	8	38	42	22
Stockport County	21	6	9	6	31	28	21
Oxford United	21	8	5	8	34	32	21
Lincoln City	21	8	5	8	28	37	21
Chesterfield	18	7	6	5	23	21	20
Bradford City	20	8	4	8	30	31	20
Doncaster Rovers	21	7	6	8	33	36	20
Darlington	20	6	8	6	25	32	20
Rochdale	19	6	7	6	28	21	19
Halifax Town	21	5	9	8	38	37	19
Newport County	20	7	5	8	32	33	19
York City	21	6	4	11	25	28	16
Tranmere Rovers	20	5	6	9	29	37	16
Southport	21	5	5	11	27	41	15
Bradford P.A.	21	4	6	11	35	47	14
Barrow	18	3	8	7	21	34	14
Hartlepools United	19	4	5	10	18	42	13

WESTERN LEAGUE

	P	W	D	L	F	A	Pts
Torquay United	19	10	3	6	46	28	23
Bideford	14	10	2	2	38	12	22
Bristol City	14	9	4	1	40	15	22
Welton Rovers	16	10	2	4	34	19	22
Bridgwater Town	12	10	0	2	22	10	20
Andover	15	7	4	4	40	32	18
Yeovil Town	17	6	6	5	32	34	18
Salisbury City	15	8	1	6	29	25	17
Chippenham Town	16	7	2	7	28	22	16
Minehead	12	8	0	4	25	20	16
Barnstaple Town	15	7	2	6	34	28	16
Dorchester Town	12	4	7	1	23	15	15
Weymouth	17	3	8	6	31	32	14
EXETER CITY	18	4	5	9	37	40	13
Bath City	16	4	5	7	33	39	13
Portland United	16	5	3	8	30	46	13
Glastonbury	15	5	2	8	35	41	12
Poole Town	18	5	2	11	25	37	12
Frome Town	15	4	2	9	28	45	10
Weston-Super-Mare	15	3	3	9	20	31	9
Bridport	15	2	5	8	16	38	9
Taunton Town	16	2	4	10	10	47	8

Saturday 7th December

FA CUP ROUND TWO

Yeovil's Cup heroics continued with a fantastic 3-1 home victory over Crystal Palace watched by almost 11000 fans packed into The Huish.

Torquay joined Exeter in being dumped out at home courtesy of a 3-2 defeat by Aldershot.

Kendal-based club Nethefield did well to hold Chesterfield to a draw. The replay at Saltergate was scheduled for a Wednesday afternoon kick off as the home side were one of the few League clubs still without floodlights.

The 15,000 plus crowd at the Exeter v Bristol City game was, by come distance, the largest attendance of the round.

2	07/12/63 Barnsley	Rochdale	3-1	9431
2	07/12/63 Brentford	Gravesend & Northfleet	1-0	11850
2	07/12/63 Carlisle United	Gateshead	4-3	12720
2	07/12/63 Chelmsford City	Bedford	0-1	9017
2	07/12/63 Chester	Barrow	0-2	8737
2	07/12/63 Colchester United	QPR	0-1	6481
2	07/12/63 Coventry City	Bristol Rovers	1-2	26248
2	07/12/63 Doncaster Rovers	Notts County	1-1	8810
2	07/12/63 Exeter City	Bristol City	0-2	15077
2	07/12/63 Lincoln City	Southport	2-0	6719
2	07/12/63 Luton Town	Reading	2-1	9047
2	07/12/63 Netherfield	Chesterfield	1-1	3900
2	07/12/63 Newport County	Watford	2-0	5000
2	07/12/63 Oldham Athletic	Bradford (PA)	2-0	17600
2	07/12/63 Oxford United	Kettering Town	2-1	10518
2	07/12/63 Port Vale	Workington	2-1	10286
2	07/12/63 Torquay United	Aldershot	2-3	5735
2	07/12/63 Wimbledon	Bath City	2-2	7500
2	07/12/63 Wrexham	Hull City	0-2	8186
2	07/12/63 Yeovil Town	Crystal Palace	3-1	10900

Friday 29th November 1963

Football League Game 22
Friday November 29th
St James Park
7059

Exeter City	2 v 0	Stockport County
Barnett	1	Beighton
Smyth	2	Johnston
MacDonald	3	Cuthbert
Mitchell	4	Porteous
Harvey	5	Parry
Anderson	6	Ricketts
Rees(1)	7	Ward
Banks(1)	8	Evans
Curtis	9	Ryden
Grace	10	France
Phoenix	11	Bircumshaw

IN CONTROL CITY'S IMPRESSIVE PERFORMANCE

Exeter City made more scoring chances for themselves than in any other two games put together this season.

That they did not score more from them was due partly to bad finishing, partly to bad luck and partly due to a great display of goalkeeping by Beighton.

Alan Banks, Exeter's tireless forward had a brilliant game. He was always in the thick of things and always in the Stockport goal mouth when there was danger.

Graham Rees scored a well deserved goal in the ninth minute when he nipped in between two defenders and cracked home a 20-yard shot.

The second goal came from the indomitable Banks in the 73rd minute, when running through onto a Derek Grace pass. He chipped the keeper and the ball sailed into the net.

For all the times City could have scored Stockport had just had two chances and both were dealt with capably by Alan Barnett.

Back in defence, City were as sound as ever. Stockport had plenty of the play but rarely troubled Exeter.

They often looked as if they were doing what they liked in the middle of the field, but in fact they were only doing what City wanted them to.

They discovered this each time they reached the edge of the City penalty area, they got no further.

The Grecians really were in command of the game and could easily have scored half a dozen had it not been for the display of Beighton.

Saturday 30th November 1963

Western League
Bristol City 3 Exeter City 3
Scorers: Exeter City: Spiers 3.
Exeter City team: Parkhill, Quarrington, Arbury, Rutley, Parsons, Gough, Spiers, Redwood, Riding, Symington, Ley.

Saturday 7th December 1963

FA Cup Round 2
Saturday December 7th
St James Park
15077

Exeter City	0 v 2	Bristol City
Barnett	1	Gibson
Smyth	2	Briggs
MacDonald	3	Thresher
Mitchell	4	Parr
Harvey	5	Connor
Anderson	6	Low
Rees	7	Derrick
Northcott	8	Clarke
Curtis	9	Atyeo(2)
Grace	10	Williams
Phoenix	11	Hooper

HARD WORKING PERFORMANCE, BUT CITY BOW OUT OF CUP

Bristol City proved to be the better side on the day and Exeter could not really grumble about failing to make the next round.

Nothing can detract from City's fight, or the way they settled down to work themselves back into the game after a shock five minute goal from Atyeo.

It was double unlucky when an injury to Dermot Curtis should come at a time when City seemed to be really getting into their stride.

When they failed to pull anything out of the bag by half-time, things were looking black for Exeter.

For although they appeared to show a tremendous amount of running in the second half, it looked as if Bristol were quite content to pack their defence and hang on.

The men from Ashton Gate let City get so far, but no further and the result was that Exeter wore themselves into the ground.

City began to make the odd mistake and Bristol City pounced. Atyeo made certain that it was all over with another goal two minutes from time.

The Exeter defence had played just as hard as the visitors and even more constructively, if not quite successfully.

Alan Barnett who had been rock steady throughout even saved a first half penalty when Keith Harvey brought down Clark.

Wednesday 11th December 1963

CITY SIGN ADRIAN THORNE
Exeter City today completed the signing of Plymouth Argyle winger Adrian Thorne. The former Brighton and Hove Albion player has been the target for City for some time.

Earlier in the season Exeter had a bid turned down by the Argyle directors for the player who had been transfer listed last season for £4,000.

City have, however, signed him on a contract that runs until June 1965 for the reduced fee of £1,500, of which £750 was to be paid immediately and the remainder by the end of February 1964.

Normally a left winger, he scored five goals in one game against Bristol Rovers reserves recently. He has also played at centre forward for Brighton.

Saturday 14th December 1963

Football League Game 23
Saturday December 14th
St James Park
5566

Exeter City	4 v 1	Bradford City
Barnett	1	Fisher
Smyth	2	Kelly
MacDonald	3	Ellam
Mitchell(1)	4	Stowell
Harvey	5	Smith
Anderson	6	Harland(1)
Rees	7	Swayer
Banks(1)	8	Wragg
Thorne	9	Green
Grace(1)	10	Price
Phoenix	11	Hellawell
(Ellam(og))		

CONFIDENT GRECIANS HIT FOUR

The City team was full of confidence against a Bradford City team that had not won on four of their away trips this season.

City scored four and could easily have obtained four more as they swarmed around the Bradford goal in the second half.

They had tremendous backing from the defence and once again it was a win which was the result of a solid team performance.

Alan Banks put City into a 14th minute lead. He received a long pass from Les MacDonald, raced past two defenders and thumped in an 18-yard shot.

Friday 13th December 1963

FOURTH DIVISION TABLE

	P	W	D	L	F	A	Pts
Gillingham	22	13	5	4	29	13	31
Carlisle United	22	12	5	5	55	27	29
Workington	21	11	6	4	37	30	28
Brighton & H.A.	23	10	7	6	39	26	27
EXETER CITY	22	9	8	5	23	18	26
Torquay United	22	11	3	8	48	32	25
Aldershot	22	10	4	8	46	44	24
Chester	21	9	5	7	26	20	23
Lincoln City	22	9	5	8	31	39	23
Bradford City	21	9	4	8	32	31	22
Darlington	22	7	8	7	28	36	22
Stockport County	22	6	9	7	25	23	21
Oxford United	22	8	5	9	36	35	21
Chesterfield	19	7	6	6	25	24	20
Halifax Town	22	5	10	7	38	39	20
Doncaster Rovers	22	7	6	9	33	39	20
Rochdale	20	6	7	7	28	23	19
Newport County	21	7	5	9	34	37	19
Tranmere Rovers	21	6	6	9	32	37	18
Southport	22	6	5	11	31	43	17
York City	22	6	4	12	25	32	16
Hartlepools United	20	5	5	10	22	44	15
Bradford P.A.	22	4	6	12	37	51	14
Barrow	19	3	8	8	23	43	14

WESTERN LEAGUE TABLE

	P	W	D	L	F	A	Pts
Bideford	16	12	2	2	42	12	26
Bristol City	16	9	6	1	43	18	24
Torquay United	21	10	3	8	49	34	23
Bridgwater Town	13	11	0	3	31	12	22
Welton Rovers	18	10	2	6	36	24	22
Yeovil Town	18	7	6	5	35	36	20
Barnstaple Town	17	8	3	6	40	30	19
Salisbury City	17	9	1	7	34	29	19
Andover	17	7	4	6	41	36	18
Minehead	14	9	0	5	29	26	18
Dorchester Town	14	5	7	2	27	17	17
Chippenham Town	17	7	3	7	28	22	17
Weymouth	18	4	8	6	34	33	16
Poole Town	20	7	2	11	31	38	16
Bath City	18	5	5	8	37	46	15
EXETER CITY	20	4	6	10	40	51	14
Glastonbury	17	5	3	9	38	45	13
Weston-Super-Mare	17	5	3	9	26	34	13
Portland United	17	5	3	9	32	50	13
Frome Town	17	5	2	10	30	48	12
Taunton Town	18	3	4	11	12	52	10
Bridport	15	2	5	8	16	38	9

Whiteways all ways

The rest of the goals came quickly. Arnold Mitchell first timed a 37th minute shot past Fisher.

Derek Grace netted with a good 48th minute shot, then two minutes later Banks worried Ellam into pushing into his own net.

The visitors goal came in the 78th minute from the penalty spot by Harland after Keith Harvey had fouled Green.

Debutant Adrian Thorne looked a useful midfield player and showed possibilities of a powerful shot.

It is developing into a real dog fight for the top places in the Fourth Division. No team can drop points at home and on this showing Exeter City have very little to worry about.

WESTERN LEAGUE
Weymouth 4 Exeter City 1
Scorers: Weymouth: Foxley 2, Tizard, Mulcairn. Exeter City: Spiers.

CITY SNIPPET
The Exeter City directors have decided to suspend the operation of the Development Fund for a short period, pending reorganisation. The directors take this opportunity to thank the various Agents and Supporters who have contributed to the Fund in the past, and trust that this same support will be forthcoming when the Fund recommences.

Wednesday 18th December 1963

F.A. YOUTH CUP ROUND TWO
Plymouth Argyle 3 Exeter City 1
Scorer: Exeter City: Ley
Exeter City team: May, Quarrington, Arbury, Rutley, Edmunds, Pope, Barnes, Symington, Redwood, Ley, Stuckey.

Thursday 19th December 1963

CITY SNIPPET
Exeter City had been approached by British United Airways who were interested in advertising on the roof of the grandstand at St James' Park.

Lincoln City

VERSUS

EXETER CITY

SATURDAY, 21st DECEMBER, 1963

Kick-off 3 p.m.

OFFICIAL PROGRAMME — 3d

The Holder of the Winning Number of this Issue of Programme will be paid £1. Please call at Secretary's Office after the Match to receive money

Nº 580

Saturday 21st December 1963

Football League Game 24
Saturday December 21st
Sincil Bank
3673

Lincoln City	1 v 1	Exeter City
Carling	1	Barnett
Jones	2	Smyth
Smith	3	MacDonald
Linnecar	4	Mitchell
Howard	5	Harvey
Neal(1)	6	Anderson
Holmes	7	Rees
Milner	8	Banks
Houghton	9	Thorne
Morton	10	Grace(1)
Campbell	11	Phoenix

CITY EARN A POINT IN THE SNOW

The bone hard pitch with its light and patchy covering of snow was certainly playable, but it was one of those days that lion hearted challenges and sliding tackles were definitely ruled out.

So it says a lot for the players of both sides that they were still able to make a match fast enough and demanding enough to draw the supporters minds away from their seemingly fast freezing feet.

It was natural enough that were mistakes, with players sliding about on the frozen surface.

City grabbed an early lead as Derek Grace nodded in a Peter Phoenix corner after just ten minutes.

The first half was definitely in Exeter's favour. They played neat football and their attacks were always incisive efforts.

The second half was tactically Lincoln City's, because they hardly ever stopped surging towards the Exeter goal, often using an eight man attack which almost turned the game their way.

City did not shatter under the storm though, however they cracked once 15 minutes from time, when Neal raced up to head in a left wing cross.

But one goal conceded was not only understandable, but it was also excusable in view of the conditions.

Better still Exeter made a comeback after that goal and only a desperately out flung foot from Carling stopped Keith Harvey's shot being the winner.

WESTERN LEAGUE
Exeter City 2 Salisbury City 2
Scorers: Exeter City: Riding, Henderson. Salisbury City: Henderson, Cranmer.
Exeter City team: Parkhill, Quarrington, Patrick, Rutley, Northcott, Gough, Riding, Symington, Henderson, Edgar, Ley.

Salisbury City team: Stevens, Pugsley, Collins, Prosser, Compton, Palmer, Cranmer, Ambrose, Henderson, Pierce, Bevan.

Tuesday December 24th

NORTHCOTT RETURNS TO CHELTENHAM
George Northcott has re-signed for Southern League Cheltenham Town, the club he left for Exeter City at the start of the season.

Northcott, who played his last match for the Grecians in the 2-2 draw at home to Salisbury City in a Western League fixture on Saturday, wanted regular first team football.

Cheltenham were keen to take back their former player and therefore Exeter decided not to stand in his way.

CITY PLAYERS HAVE NEVER HAD IT SO GOOD
When you consider what players used to have to go through at Christmas only a few years ago, then you realise that like most other occupations the professional footballer has never had it so good.

Three games in Christmas week used to be a common occurrence, but when studying the records you are astonished to find that in season 1910-11, Exeter City's first team, who were then competing in the Southern League, had to play four games in five days, and six games in eight days!

Professional footballers then used to earn around £3 to £4 per week, but then it was possible to buy a new pair of the very best football boots for only 8s 6d!

Thursday 26th December 1963

Football League Game 25
Thursday December 26th
Goldstone Ground
10250

Brighton & H Albion	1 v 2	Exeter City
Powney	1	Barnett
Sanders	2	Smyth
Jennings	3	MacDonald
Bertolini	4	Mitchell
Gall	5	Harvey
Turner	6	Anderson
Cooper	7	Rees
Collins	8	Banks(1)
Webber	9	Thorne(1)
Healer(1)	10	Grace
Goodchild	11	Phoenix

HAPPY CHRISTMAS EXETER CITY!

There was certainly not a flat after Christmas atmosphere about Exeter City following this result.

From the moment former Brighton and Hove Albion player Adrian Thorne streaked through the mud just after the interval to make the score 1-1, Exeter took

BRIGHTON AND HOVE ALBION
FOOTBALL CLUB
GOLDSTONE GROUND · HOVE

SEASON 1963-64
FOOTBALL LEAGUE DIVISION IV
ALBION v EXETER CITY
THURSDAY, 26th DECEMBER, 1963   K.O. 3.0 p.m.

A SURE WINNER EVERY SATURDAY

Evening Argus
CLASSIFIED EDITION

FOOTBALL RESULTS
POOLS CHECK · LEAGUE TABLES

★ *Place a Firm Order with Your Newsagent*

PROGRAMME SIXPENCE

the initiative.

The home side, so dominant in the first half, were forced to back pedal anxiously as City went flat out for a win and with only five minutes remaining Alan Banks seized his chance.

Alan Barnett, Cecil Smyth and Keith Harvey had been particularly busy in the opening half hour. Barnett bringing off many spectacular saves.

Brighton's goal followed a furious bombardment, with Healer scoring from close range.

However, Thorne's enterprise and marksmanship was something that Brighton simply couldn't match as he made a triumphant return to the Goldstone Ground.

Thorne received good support from his wingers. Peter Phoenix in particular sending through many accurate passes in the closing stages.

Whilst Arnold Mitchell was also able to move upfield, join and support City's attacking moves.

The home players were given the slow handclap as they strove to recapture their snap of the first half.

WESTERN LEAGUE
Exeter City 1 Bristol City 4
With Bristol City set to take the points, the match was abandoned due to the ever thickening fog around St James' Park. George Spiers netted for the Grecians.

Saturday 28th December 1963

Football League Game 26
Saturday December 28th
St James Park
9875

Exeter City	0 v 0	Brighton & H Albion
Barnett	1	Powney
Smyth	2	Sanders
MacDonald	3	Jennings
Mitchell	4	Bertolini
Harvey	5	Burtenshaw
Anderson	6	Turner
Rees	7	Cooper
Banks	8	Collins
Thorne	9	Webber
Grace	10	Jackson
Phoenix	11	Goodchild

A BATTLING GOALLESS DRAW

In a game with all the hectic action of a promotion battle, but little calm, constructive football, Exeter City and Brighton and Hove Albion battled it out to a goalless draw.

Brighton never let City settle into their smooth stride, with a tough, determined display. They tackled quickly with fearsome power that shook some of the City players.

The Exeter forwards seldom showed the bright ideas or sudden bursts of speed

Friday 3rd January 1964

FOURTH DIVISION TABLE

	P	W	D	L	F	A	Pts
Gillingham	26	16	5	5	38	15	37
Carlisle United	26	15	6	5	71	33	36
EXETER CITY	26	11	10	5	30	19	32
Workington	25	12	7	6	42	37	31
Torquay United	26	12	4	10	52	38	28
Brighton & H.A.	27	10	8	9	41	31	28
Oxford United	26	11	6	9	41	36	28
Aldershot	26	12	4	10	54	49	28
Lincoln City	26	11	6	9	36	41	28
Chester	25	11	5	9	31	26	27
Darlington	25	9	8	8	35	45	26
Rochdale	23	9	7	7	36	25	25
Stockport County	25	8	9	8	30	29	25
Newport County	25	10	5	10	39	41	25
Bradford City	24	10	4	10	36	37	24
Doncaster Rovers	26	9	6	11	40	44	24
Halifax Town	25	6	10	9	42	46	22
Tranmere Rovers	25	7	8	10	39	45	22
Southport	26	8	5	13	36	51	21
Chesterfield	23	7	6	10	27	32	20
Bradford P.A.	26	6	6	14	40	56	18
Hartlepools United	24	6	5	13	26	52	17
York City	25	6	4	15	27	40	16
Barrow	23	3	10	10	26	47	16

WESTERN LEAGUE TABLE

	P	W	D	L	F	A	Pts
Bideford	20	15	3	2	55	16	33
Bristol City	19	11	7	1	57	19	29
Bridgwater Town	18	13	2	3	39	14	28
Welton Rovers	21	13	2	6	41	25	28
Barnstaple Town	21	11	3	7	50	33	25
Torquay United	23	11	3	9	51	37	25
Yeovil Town	23	9	6	8	41	57	24
Andover	21	8	6	7	45	39	22
Salisbury City	20	10	2	8	38	33	22
Dorchester Town	18	7	7	4	33	23	21
Minehead	18	10	1	7	39	40	21
Chippenham Town	20	8	3	9	31	24	19
Weymouth	21	5	9	7	43	40	19
Poole Town	24	8	3	13	34	44	19
Weston-Super-Mare	20	7	4	9	30	34	18
Bath City	21	5	7	9	41	55	17
Frome Town	20	7	3	10	36	51	17
Glastonbury	21	6	3	12	43	54	15
EXETER CITY	23	4	7	12	43	60	15
Portland United	21	6	3	12	38	58	15
Taunton Town	21	4	4	13	14	57	12
Bridport	20	2	6	12	21	50	10

F. A. BRIDGES & SON LTD.

Building Contractors & Decorators

Specialists in —

HIGH-CLASS JOINERY
FRENCH POLISHING

FRANCIS CLOSE, WARDREW ROAD, EXETER Tel. 74536

that might have enabled them to pierce Brighton's strong defence.

They seemed jaded and even Alan Banks found it impossible to slip away from his shadow like marking.

Adrian Thorne was guilty of a terrible miss lofting the ball over an open goal from five yards, with the goalkeeper on the ground.

All the outstanding performances were in the City defence. Everyone expects Keith Harvey to play well in every game and this time he excelled himself.

Des Anderson saw a tremendous amount of action, while Les MacDonald seems to be back to his best form.

The only time that Brighton did manage to pierce the City rearguard, Collins rattled the crossbar with a 25-yard shot.

WESTERN LEAGUE
Barnstaple Town 3 Exeter City 0
Scorers: Barnstaple Town: Pulman 2, Wardle.

CITY MANAGER NOW CHIEF SCOUT
Former Exeter City player-manager Norman Kirkman is now chief scout for Southampton. Kirkman was in charge of the Grecians between March 1952 and March 1953, having been signed from Southampton, before moving on to take charge of Bradford Park Avenue.

Saturday 4th January 1964

Football League Game 27
Saturday January 4th
St James Park
7286

Exeter City	2 v 1	Workington
Barnett	1	Ower
Smyth	2	Johnston
MacDonald	3	Lumsden
Mitchell	4	Furphy
Harvey	5	Brown
Anderson	6	Burkinshaw
Rees	7	Middlesmass
Banks(1)	8	Carr
Thorne	9	Commons(1)
Grace(1)	10	Moran
Ley	11	Martin

FOURTH DIVISION FOOTBALL AT ITS VERY BEST

This victory gave the St James' Park supporters skill, thrills and 90 minutes of the very best entertainment value that the Fourth Division can provide.

It takes two sides to make a good match and Workington got right down to their contribution with a goal after only 8 minutes from Commons.

As supporters shouted themselves hoarse, Exeter grabbed a 16th minute equaliser from Alan Banks and a 68th minute winner from a Derek Grace header.

The win itself was important, almost vital, for with Workington just one league place and one point behind it was worth double its normal points value to Exeter City.

Faced with a tough, fast and competent northern line up and playing under the handicap of the early goal, City rolled up their sleeves and got down to work with a ferocity not seen for some time.

They displayed team work and effort in abundance to produce a fine performance against equally tough opposition.

CITY'S FINE DEFENSIVE RECORD
Currently the only club in the Fourth Division with a better defensive record than Exeter City is Gillingham.

If City's present average is maintained, it could mean that they would only concede 33 goals in 46 matches, and that would easily be the best in the history of the club.

It is a fantastic figure when you consider that the present Fourth Division record in 47 goals in 46 games by Coventry City in 1958-59.

It is worth noting that prior to the fixture against Workington at St. James' Park, that there have only been four Fourth Division games this season in which City have conceded more than one goal, and they have kept their goal intact on no less than 12 occasions.

No visiting side has succeeded in scoring more than one goal in a league game at St. James' Park since promotion winning Brentford netted twice in a draw that rounded off the 1962-63 campaign at home.

WESTERN LEAGUE
Minehead 2 Exeter City 0
Exeter City team: Parkhill, Rutley, Patrick, Henderson, Parsons, Gough, Welsh, Stuckey, Riding, Symington, Spiers

Friday 10th January 1964

CITY APPOINT NEW DIRECTOR
There will be one new face at the Exeter City versus Gillingham game tomorrow as Fred Dart, a Shaldon businessman takes his place in the directors box.

Dart was voted onto the board of Exeter City F.C. at last night's board meeting, having purchased the agreed amount of shares, and also making loan of a cash sum to the club.

Friday 10th January 1964

FOURTH DIVISION TABLE

	P	W	D	L	F	A	Pts
Gillingham	27	16	6	5	38	15	38
Carlisle United	26	15	6	5	71	33	36
EXETER CITY	27	12	10	5	32	20	34
Workington	26	12	7	7	43	39	31
Torquay United	26	12	4	10	52	28	28
Brighton & H.A.	27	10	8	9	41	31	28
Chester	26	11	6	9	34	29	28
Oxford United	26	11	6	9	41	36	28
Aldershot	26	12	4	10	54	49	28
Lincoln City	26	11	6	9	36	41	28
Darlington	27	10	8	9	39	48	28
Stockport County	26	9	9	8	33	31	27
Rochdale	24	9	8	7	36	25	26
Bradford City	25	11	4	10	39	39	26
Newport County	25	10	5	10	39	41	25
Tranmere Rovers	27	8	9	10	45	49	25
Doncaster Rovers	26	9	6	11	40	44	24
Halifax Town	25	6	10	9	42	46	22
Southport	26	8	5	13	36	51	21
Chesterfield	24	7	6	11	29	37	20
Bradford P.A.	27	6	6	15	41	59	18
Barrow	24	4	10	10	31	49	18
Hartlepools United	25	6	5	14	26	54	17
York City	26	6	4	16	29	43	16

WESTERN LEAGUE TABLE

	P	W	D	L	F	A	Pts
Bideford	21	15	3	3	56	18	33
Bristol City	20	12	7	1	58	19	31
Bridgwater Town	19	14	2	3	41	15	30
Welton Rovers	21	13	2	6	41	25	28
Barnstaple Town	22	11	4	7	50	33	26
Torquay United	23	11	3	9	51	37	25
Yeovil Town	23	9	6	8	41	57	24
Salisbury City	21	10	3	8	39	34	23
Minehead	19	11	1	7	41	40	23
Andover	22	8	6	8	46	41	22
Dorchester Town	18	7	7	4	33	23	21
Chippenham Town	21	8	4	9	32	25	20
Weymouth	22	5	10	7	44	41	20
Weston-Super-Mare	21	7	5	9	30	34	19
Poole Town	25	8	3	14	35	46	19
Frome Town	21	7	4	10	37	52	18
Glastonbury	22	7	3	12	45	55	17
Bath City	22	5	7	10	43	58	17
EXETER CITY	24	4	7	13	43	62	15
Portland United 22	22	6	3	13	38	59	15
Taunton Town	22	5	4	13	17	59	14
Bridport	21	3	6	12	23	51	12

MATTHEWS BEERS SPIRITS

For Celebrations of all kinds we can offer the best selection in the City. Glasses, etc., loaned free of charge. Free delivery and collection

WINES

40, Sidwell Street, Exeter   **Tel. 54689**

Saturday 11th January 1964

Football League Game 28
Saturday January 11th
St James Park
10905

Exeter City	0 v 0	Gillingham
Barnett	1	Simpson
Smyth	2	Hudson
MacDonald	3	Hunt
Mitchell	4	Arnott
Harvey	5	Burgess
Anderson	6	Farrall
Rees	7	Ballagher
Banks	8	Yeo
Thorne	9	White
Curtis	10	Gibbs
Grace	11	Newman

FRUSTRATING STALEMATE AT THE PARK

Gillingham came to St James' Park with the best defensive record in the entire Football League and they certainly lived up to that reputation.

Whether you like the method of achieving that is another thing entirely, but they were certainly effective.

The slightest hint of danger and they passed back to goalkeeper Simpson. It slowed down the play, but was very frustrating to watch.

Apart from one Adrian Thorne shot and a header from Alan Banks, City were foiled every time.

It was a game that had its share of fireworks and at times there were only inches between City's desperate efforts and a match winning goal.

Dermot Curtis, Banks and Thorne all weaved and darted around trying to find the vital gap, but Gillingham covered quickly and the openings were scarce.

City's defence came out better than Gillingham's, because it was just as safe without being so time wasting and crude.

They gave very little away and only shots from Yeo and Newman looked at all like getting a goal.

Cecil Smyth and Les MacDonald played very well, but again it was a team effort that got City through.

WESTERN LEAGUE
Frome Town 1 Exeter City 1
Scorers: Frome Town: Cribb. Exeter City: Howells
Exeter City team: Thompson, Quarrington, Patrick, Rutley, Parsons, Howells, Welsh, Edgar, Riding, Gough, Spiers.
Playing in goal for the Grecians in this match was a 15-year-old trialist, Bob Thompson, who came from Aldershot.

NEW INCENTIVE FOR CITY PLAYERS

Until this week, the Exeter City players have received an ten shillings in their wage packets for every complete 500 additional spectators over 5,000.

As from the game against Gillingham, the incentive scheme has been changed with the new deal giving them an additional payment of £10 each week as long as they remain in the top four places in the Fourth Division. They would also receive an additional £10 per week if the team were top of the table.

This applies to both home and way games unlike the old scheme, and it was reported that the players were extremely happy with the new arrangement as it would mean a big increase over the old scheme.

Saturday 18th January 1964

Football League Game 29
Saturday January 18th
Haig Avenue
1618

Southport	1 v 1	Exeter City
Rollo	1	Barnett
Cairns	2	Smyth
Beanland	3	MacDonald
Rutherford	4	Mitchell
Wallace	5	Harvey
Tighe	6	Anderson
Dagger	7	Rees
Russell	8	Banks(1)
Ambler	9	Curtis
Spence(1)	10	Grace
Peat	11	Thorne

GREAT START THEN PEGGED BACK

Everything went to plan for Exeter City on a frost bound pitch. They could not have got off to better start as they scored after only 60 seconds through Alan Banks.

They played neat push and run football and held the lead comfortably at half-time. In the second half though, Southport proved to be a different side.

The hosts tackled harder, and upset City's usual style, and then started to cut Exeter to shreds.

Spence equalised in the 57th minute and but for two brilliant saves from Alan Barnett he would have scored again.

Southport tore into City and the normally reliable defensive marking began to slip and so did their too close clearances, so that Exeter's forwards did not have enough force to get them out of their own half more than a mere handful of times.

Even so, City should have had the game sewn up in the first half when they had Southport's defence running all ways and making mistakes.

A point away from home is of course always a good one and especially precious in City's position. but this could and should have been two for them.

If this is an example of their general form in a freeze up, and it was truly freezing at Southport, then lets hope for a thaw, for they have two more trips North in the next two weeks.

WESTERN LEAGUE
Exeter City 2 Bridport 1
Scorers: Exeter City: Riding, Rutley. Bridport: Donovan.

Wednesday 22nd January 1964

PHOENIX LEAVES CITY
Exeter City winger Peter Phoenix is to sign for Southport for a fee of £625. He only joined the Grecians last October from Rochdale, but he has missed the North of England and his friends there.

He took only a few hours to make up his mind to Join Southport when he became aware they were interested in signing him.

Phoenix has made 15 league appearances and scored one goal in his brief spell at St James' Park.

Saturday 25th January 1964

Football League Game 30
Saturday January 25th
Park Avenue
6273

Bradford (Park Avenue)	3 v 2	Exeter City
Hardie	1	Barnett
Thomas	2	Smyth
Jones	3	MacDonald
Cock	4	Mitchell
McCalman	5	Harvey
Flynn	6	Anderson
Burns	7	Rees
Spratt(1)	8	Banks(1)
Atkinson	9	Henderson
Hector(1)	10	Grace(1)
Bird(1)	11	Thorne

MISSED CHANCES AND CITY PAY THE PENALTY

Although Exeter City lost this game, there was no lack of fight, for they played as well as in the majority of matches this season. The big fault was the missing of three chances.

In a good game, Bradford played well above their lowly position, and while City did almost everything they could, Bradford did better.

They played with a four man defence so City's tactics of working the ball around until they could find a gap and then making a quick breakthrough were obviously right.

Spratt who was given a second chance as he collected the rebound off his first shot gave Bradford a fourth minute lead.

But once City got going they had two thirds of the play and after Graham Rees had hit a post, Alan Banks got a well deserved equaliser.

Faster to the ball and more accurate, Exeter looked the better side, but their finishing let them down.

Derek Grace got a 49th minute goal to give them the lead, but mid way through the second half, Bird netted an equaliser.

City continued to miss chances, with Adrian Thorne and Alan Banks the culprits, both when well placed.

Exeter paid dearly for not scoring when Hector stole in to hit the Bradford winner twenty minutes from time.

In the simplest forms this was a game that was lost and no amount of analytical discussion will bring a really satisfactory answer, or save the points now

WESTERN LEAGUE
Exeter City 3 Taunton Town 1
Scorers: Exeter City: Quarrington, Riding, Curtis. Taunton Town: Barnes.
Exeter City team: Parkhill, Quarrington, Patrick, Rutley, Parsons, Welsh, Riding, Redwood, Curtis, Edgar, Ley.
Taunton Town team: Stone, Thomas, Whitnall, Sage, Deplidge, Harrison, Court, Milson, Barnes, Clarke, Bailey.

Saturday 1st February 1964

GIFT GOAL DEFEATS CITY

Another two possible promotion points went down the drain at Doncaster Rovers, as Exeter City gave away the only goal of the game and failed to fight back.

The goal in the 14th minute was the result of a terrible goal kick by Alan Barnett. It went straight to Booth who whacked it back into the net. A gift goal.

Exeter had to play into a gale force wind and at half time they looked as if they would be able to at least equalise, if not win the game, with the elements in their favour after the interval.

Football League Game 31
Saturday February 1st
Park Avenue
8083

Doncaster Rovers	1 v 0	Exeter City
Potter	1	Barnett
Raine	2	Patrick
Meadows	3	MacDonald
Windross	4	Mitchell
White	5	Harvey
Ripley	6	Anderson
Robinson	7	Curtis
Booth(1)	8	Banks
Hale	9	Thorne
Jeffrey	10	Grace
Broadbent	11	Rees

Instead of using the long ball which was the most effective pass with the help of the wind, City persisted in the short passing game, and lone challenges from Alan Banks, who almost wore himself out chasing lost cases without support.

When allowed, Doncaster settled down and forced City back and it was only a matter of bad luck that they did not score again.

City's defence did not look very secure. Gaps began to appear and when the forwards did get the ball, they didn't hold it long enough. Consequently the defence was under much pressure.

In the whole of the second half City managed just two shots at goal, while the Grecian goal mouth looked like a shooting gallery.

WESTERN LEAGUE
Exeter City 6 Glastonbury 2
Scorers: Exeter City: Riding 5, Spiers.
Exeter City team: Thompson, Quarrington, Gough, Spiers, Parsons, Rutley, Welsh, Edgar, Riding, Henderson, Ley.

Monday 3rd February 1964

GEORGE GILBERT RETIRES AGAIN
Former long serving club secretary, George Gilbert has retired from his work in the Exeter City F.C. offices.

He came out of retirement to work for the Development Fund Lottery which commenced last season.

Now that the Fund has closed down, although City chairman Reg Rose has said that it is temporarily suspended, Gilbert has retired again.

He is, however, willing to come back and help City out again should they require him at any time.

Friday 7th February 1964

FOURTH DIVISION TABLE

	P	W	D	L	F	A	Pts
Gillingham	30	17	8	5	41	16	42
Carlisle United	30	17	6	7	76	38	40
Workington	30	14	9	7	49	41	37
EXETER CITY	31	12	12	7	35	25	36
Bradford City	31	16	4	11	48	46	36
Torquay United	30	15	5	10	59	40	35
Chester	30	14	6	10	42	36	34
Lincoln City	30	13	7	10	42	47	33
Tranmere Rovers	31	11	10	10	55	50	32
Brighton & H.A.	31	10	10	11	43	35	30
Oxford United	29	11	8	10	42	36	30
Oxford United	29	11	8	10	42	36	30
Stockport County	31	10	10	11	38	39	30
Doncaster Rovers	30	11	7	12	53	48	29
Aldershot	29	12	5	12	54	55	29
Darlington	31	10	9	12	42	64	29
Rochdale	27	9	9	9	37	30	27
Newport County	28	11	5	12	42	45	27
Bradford P.A.	31	10	6	15	52	62	26
Southport	30	10	6	14	44	56	26
Chesterfield	28	9	7	12	32	40	25
Halifax Town	29	6	11	12	45	54	23
Barrow	28	4	12	12	34	56	20
York City	30	7	5	18	33	47	19
Hartlepools United	29	7	5	17	31	61	19

WESTERN LEAGUE TABLE

	P	W	D	L	F	A	Pts
Bideford	25	17	4	4	64	26	38
Bridgwater Town	23	17	3	3	48	16	37
Bristol City	24	13	10	1	65	24	36
Welton Rovers	24	14	3	7	45	29	31
Barnstaple Town	26	12	6	8	54	38	30
Andover	26	10	8	8	56	44	28
Salisbury City	25	12	4	9	49	44	28
Yeovil Town	27	11	6	10	46	64	28
Torquay United	27	12	3	12	58	47	27
Minehead	22	13	1	8	49	47	27
Dorchester Town	22	9	7	6	41	30	25
Weymouth	26	7	11	8	55	51	25
Chippenham Town	25	9	4	12	43	35	22
EXETER CITY	28	7	8	13	55	67	22
Poole Town	29	8	6	15	40	55	22
Weston-Super-Mare	25	8	5	12	36	43	21
Bath City	25	6	9	10	47	60	21
Frome Town	25	8	5	12	42	57	21
Glastonbury	26	7	4	15	49	68	18
Portland United	25	7	3	15	48	72	17
Taunton Town	26	5	6	15	22	67	16
Bridport	23	4	6	13	25	53	14

For **ESSO** Petrols and Oils

Exeter Service Station
F. BATCHELOR
BY-PASS

★

Middlemoor Service Station
W. R. ROWE
SIDMOUTH ROAD

EXETER
DEVON, Telephone 76148

ESSO DEALER
WIDE STOCK OF ACCESSORIES
7-DAY SERVICE

Friday 7th February 1964

CITY WOBBLE
Two defeats and some of the worriers amongst Exeter City supporters are already beginning to lengthen the odds against winning promotion.

True, one point from three away games isn't promotion form, but Workington, the team that has overtaken City in the table, had a run of four away defeats before they got a point at Barrow three weeks ago. It doesn't seem to have shaken their promotion chances.

At the moment the Grecians are still only one point behind that promotion ideal of one point from each away game, and indeed, only two clubs in the Fourth Division, Gillingham and Carlisle United, have so far been able to maintain that rate.

Gillingham, Carlisle United, Workington and Exeter City have now been among the top six places since the middle of October, and during this time the most consistent challengers for these promotion places have been Torquay United, Chester and Lincoln City.

It seems like that the climax of Exeter City's season will be the Easter games against Torquay. Promotion for either club may hinge on the result of those fixtures.

Saturday 8th February 1964

Football League Game 32
Saturday February 8th
St James Park
6077

Exeter City	2 v 1	**Hartlepools United**
Barnett	1	Oakley
Patrick	2	Bilclif
MacDonald	3	Stonehouse
Mitchell	4	Johnson
Harvey	5	Fraser
Anderson	6	Hinshelwood
Rees(1)	7	Hinchcliffe
Banks(1)	8	Fogarty
Henderson	9	Thompson(1)
Grace	10	Bradley
Thorne	11	Burlison

REES GRABS LATE WINNER

The Liverpool sound has certainly come to St James' Park since the signing of Alan Banks, but unfortunately it is the sound of a one man band, for maestro Banks has wound up playing all five forward arrangements on his own.

Exeter won, but it could have so easily been 6-1 instead of 2-1, and if it had not been for Banks, who did all of the work, they may not have won at all.

Banks was often the lone attacker. He ran himself into the ground with 100 per cent effort and got a goal as well.

The game itself was nothing to write home about. Exeter had almost all of the play against a weak, but desperate Hartlepool, but it was often, slow, stodgy stuff, that was comparable with the surface it was played on.

Banks got the City in front after 27 minutes. John Henderson had a shot blocked on the line, but that was about it in a poor first half.

The second half was only a few minutes old when the inevitable happened. Inevitable because the City had not crushed the Northerners as they should have done, and they still had enough spark in them to grab a goal from Thompson.

Then after some City supporters had already gone home in disgust, Graham Rees bobbed up four minutes from time to crack the winner.

WESTERN LEAGUE
Andover 3 Exeter City 1
Scorers: Andover: Allen, Brown, Hall. Exeter City: Ley.
Exeter City team: Parkhill, Smyth, Quarrington, Spiers, Rutley, Gough, Welsh, Redwood, Riding, Edgar, Ley.

Monday 10th February 1964

EDWARDS NOT IMPRESSED
Friendly
Poole Town 0 Exeter City 1
Scorer: Exeter City: Riding.
Exeter City team: Parkhill, Smyth, MacDonald, Spiers, Harvey, Gough, Welsh, Riding, Curtis, Edgar, Ley.

"Nothing new," was manager Jack Edwards comment after Exeter City's friendly fixture at Poole Town, when amateur forward, Alan Riding got the only goal of the game.

Edwards was not impressed by the rest of the attack despite the players having the chance to shine and stake a place in the first team for their fixture at Darlington on Saturday.

Exeter City had agreed to the friendly fixture at Poole, subject to them keeping 50% of the gate receipts to offset any expenses that they had incurred.

Wednesday 12th February 1964

PROGRAMME ADVERTISEMENTS
Exeter City have agreed a contract with Allsports Publicity Co. Ltd who will be responsible for the advertising in the match programme.

In return Allsports would be paying a fee of £500 per season to the Grecians, the

Darlington F.C.

Programme Price 3d.

John Neasham Ltd.

MAIN FORD DEALER

DARLINGTON 5387-8
NORTHALLERTON 621-2   RICHMOND 3073-4

Saturday, 15th February, 1964   v. EXETER CITY

BIG OR SMALL
WE SERVE THEM ALL!

Petrols, Fuel Oils and Greases

MAJOR & COMPANY LTD.

Your local depot: Sunderland 4368

Head Office: Sculcoates, Hull
Tel.: 20715/4 and 32926

contract being for three years as from the start of the 1964-65 season, with an option to extend it by a further two years.

Saturday 15th February 1964

Football League Game 33
Saturday February 15th
Feethams
2647

Darlington	1 v 1	Exeter City
Penman	1	Barnett
Peverall	2	Smyth
Storton	3	MacDonald
Atkinson	4	Mitchell
D Robson	5	Harvey
Duffy	6	Anderson
Rayment	7	Rees(1)
Lawton	8	Banks
L Robson(1)	9	Thorne
Allison	10	Grace
McGeochie	11	Ley

ANOTHER LATE GOAL EARNS CITY A POINT

There were several factors against Exeter City, the rough and tumble tactics of Darlington, the occasional bad run of the ball at a vital moment, and the sometimes baffling decisions and indecisions of the officials.

They all went against City giving a proper account of themselves, at the same time one always had the feeling that they should be doing just a little better.

In the first half, City were helped by an injury to Darlington's left back, Storton, and Exeter raided down the left side.

George Ley had a goal ruled out for offside. Graham Rees hit a post and Alan Banks had a lob miraculously headed out from under the bar.

In the second half, Darlington packed their defence. City still had most of the play, but it came to a halt when they reached the penalty area as they tried to equalise Darlington's first minute goal from Robson.

Then for the second successive week City were saved by a Rees goal, with a neat header from an Adrian Thorne cross with just four minutes remaining.

It was close, too close for comfort, but it was well deserved. Cecil Smyth was back in defence after two weeks rest and played as well as ever, and certainly as efficiently as any other defender on the field.

WESTERN LEAGUE
Exeter City 2 Torquay United 2
Scorers: Exeter City: Riding, Curtis. Torquay United: Richardson, Evans.
Exeter City team: Parkhill, Quarrington, Spiers, Edgar, Parsons, Gough, Welsh, Riding, Curtis, Henderson, Stuckey.
Torquay United team: Barnsley, Rossiter, Balsom, Austin, Dusting, Hancock, Evans, Cox, Richardson, Murphy, Tolchard.

Friday 21st February 1964

FOURTH DIVISION TABLE

	P	W	D	L	F	A	Pts
Gillingham	32	17	10	5	43	18	44
Carlisle United	31	17	6	8	78	41	40
EXETER CITY	33	13	13	7	38	27	39
Workington	32	15	9	8	54	43	39
Bradford City	32	17	4	11	50	47	38
Torquay United	32	15	6	11	62	44	36
Chester	32	15	6	11	48	41	36
Lincoln City	32	14	8	10	48	49	36
Tranmere Rovers	33	12	11	10	59	52	36
Brighton & H.A.	33	12	10	11	51	36	34
Stockport County	33	12	10	11	41	40	34
Oxford United	30	12	8	10	44	39	32
Doncaster Rovers	32	12	7	13	56	54	31
Aldershot	31	13	5	13	56	54	31
Darlington	33	10	10	13	44	68	30
Newport County	29	12	5	12	43	45	29
Bradford P.A.	33	11	6	16	53	64	28
Southport	32	11	6	15	47	59	28
Rochdale	29	9	9	11	37	32	27
Chesterfield	30	10	7	13	35	44	27
Halifax Town	31	6	12	13	45	58	24
York City	32	8	5	19	35	48	21
Barrow	30	4	12	14	35	59	20
Hartlepools United	31	7	5	19	33	67	19

WESTERN LEAGUE TABLE

	P	W	D	L	F	A	Pts
Bideford	27	19	4	4	71	28	42
Bridgwater Town	25	19	3	3	54	16	41
Bristol City	25	14	10	1	70	25	38
Barnstaple Town	28	14	6	8	63	39	34
Andover	28	12	8	8	62	45	32
Welton Rovers	26	14	3	9	46	37	31
Salisbury City	27	13	5	9	53	45	31
Torquay United	29	13	4	12	63	49	30
Yeovil Town	29	12	6	11	48	66	30
Dorchester Town	24	11	7	6	49	33	29
Weymouth	28	8	11	9	62	56	27
Minehead	24	13	1	10	52	55	27
Chippenham Town	27	10	4	13	47	37	24
Weston-Super-Mare	27	9	6	13	41	45	24
Bath City	27	7	9	11	53	64	23
EXETER CITY	30	7	9	14	58	72	23
Poole Town	31	8	6	17	43	63	22
Frome Town	27	8	5	14	43	67	21
Glastonbury	27	7	5	15	50	69	19
Portland United	27	3	17	48	81	17
Taunton Town	28	5	6	17	22	74	16
Bridport	25	4	7	14	25	56	15

Tel. **74669**   Tel. **72750**

IMPERIAL HOTEL
EXETER

LUNCHEONS   DINNERS   SPECIAL FUNCTIONS
LICENSED   LARGE CAR PARK

Thursday 20th February 1964

CITY SNIPPETS
Salisbury City were showing an interest in signing City players, John Edgar and Ray Gough.

The Grecians were monitoring the availability of Torquay United's former Norwich City inside forward, Rod Richardson.

The club had been approached about the possibility of entering a team in the proposed Devon County Premier League, however, they were not interested.

Saturday 22nd February 1964

Football League Game 34
Saturday February 22nd
St James Park
6589

Exeter City	3 v 0	Chester
Barnett	1	Barton
Patrick	2	J Evans
MacDonald	3	Starkey
Mitchell(1)	4	G Evans
Harvey	5	Butler
Anderson	6	Corbishley
Thorne	7	Read
Banks(1)	8	Metcalf
Curtis	9	Talbot
Grace	10	Morris
Ley(1)	11	Humes

A GOOD ALL ROUND DISPLAY BY THE GRECIANS

This was Exeter City's best overall performance for weeks. They at last gave the impression of solidarity and once again it started back in defence which was pretty near faultless.

It was tough tackling and extremely quick covering of the defence that clamped right down on a potentially dangerous Chester attack right from the start. It was on this foundation that the City were able to build their win.

City had almost all of the play in the first half, but did not have the goals to show for it.

When the second half started City were full of fight and bustle instead of faltering through that opening period.

They foiled any hopes that Chester may have had with two quick goals. Alan Banks got the first as he bundled a Cecil Smyth cross over the line, and Arnold Mitchell got the second with a terrific 25-yard drive.

Two minutes from time, George Ley ran in just at the right moment to head his first ever Football League goal from Adrian Thorne's corner.

All three goals were deserved. Banks because of his non stop chasing and challenging. Mitchell because he gets through a tremendous amount of work every week with little praise and Ley, because it rounded off his best display in a City first team shirt.

WESTERN LEAGUE
Dorchester Town 7 Exeter City 0
Scorers: Dorchester Town: House 2, Fudge 2, Greening, McGuigan, Curtis.
Exeter City team: Thompson, Quarrington, Parsons, Rutley, Henderson, Gough, Welsh, Clark, Redwood, Edgar, Spiers.

Thursday 27th February 1964

HENDERSON AND SPIERS TRANSFER LISTED
At his own request, John Henderson, the 22-year-old Scots born forward signed by Exeter City from Charlton Athletic just over a year ago, has been placed on the transfer list.

Henderson has made 20 League appearances this season and scored six goals. However, he was played out of position at centre-half in the City reserves 7-0 thrashing at Dorchester Town last Saturday.

The Grecians are hoping they will be able to recover the transfer fee that they paid for him, and await interest from other clubs.

George Spiers has also had his request for a transfer granted by the club's board of directors.

Spiers had joined the Grecians at the start of the season from Irish League side, Crusaders.

Friday 28th February 1964
BANKS DOUBLE GIVES CITY VICTORY

York City had a fair percentage of the game and a win over a side third from bottom of the Fourth Division may not sound too great a triumph, but the City won it under two major handicaps.

One was their preparation, or lack of it. They had less than sixty minutes to loosen up for the game after travelling by train from Exeter for eight solid hours.

And two, was the penalty awarded against them in the 30th minute, when the ball seemed to bounce awkwardly against the arm of Derek Grace - a harsh decision. Scott scored with the penalty in off the post.

ARMY & NAVY STORES

FOSSGATE and PAVEMENT, YORK

OVERALLS — BOOTS — CLOTHING

PRICE 3d.　　　　　　　　　　OFFICIAL PROGRAMME

YORK CITY A.F.C.

President: Mr. W. H. SESSIONS, J.P.　　Vice-President: Mr. G. W. SHERRINGTON.
Directors: Messrs. H. F. W. KITCHIN (Chairman), A. G. D. BLUNDY, W. MASON,
F. H. MAGSON, N. J. HOPWOOD, T. W. MEEK, A. BROWN, K. LANCASTER,
T. MITCHELL and C. HULL.
Team Manager: Mr. T. LOCKIE.
Honorary Medical Officer: J. B. McKENNA, M.B., B.Ch.
Secretary and Registered Office:
G. TEASDALE, Bootham Crescent, York.　Telephone 24447 (Office), 25765 (Home).

No. 21　　　　　　　　　　FRIDAY, 28th FEBRUARY, 1964

CITY v. EXETER CITY

YORK CO-OP

The season's brilliant new
STANLEY MATTHEWS FOOTBALL BOOTS
...for a better feel of the ball—plus extra dash, lightness and comfort!

BOYS' MODEL
Black streamlined model with white facings and instep strips. White vulcanised waterproof sole with Fourteen Studs (H.18).
Sizes 2-5
Wide fitting

33/11

SPECIAL OFFER!
"ALERT" MEN'S MODEL
Black with white facings and instep straps, white or yellow laces. Black waterproof vulcanised soles and studs.
Sizes 6-11　**32/11**

Obtainable in York from the
FOOTWEAR DEPARTMENT, RAILWAY ST.

Come Co-operative Shopping

YORK CO-OPERATIVE SOCIETY LTD.

Football League Game 35
Friday February 28th
Bootham Crescent
3585

York City	1 v 2	**Exeter City**
Moor	1	Barnett
Wealthall	2	Smyth
Baker	3	MacDonald
Woods	4	Mitchell
Boyes	5	Harvey
M Scott	6	Anderson
J Scott	7	Rees
Peyton	8	Banks(2)
Goldie	9	Thorne
Rudd	10	Grace
Heron	11	Ley

Yet the City went on to win and win well. They played the better football against weak tackling and a dithering York, with Arnold Mitchell prompting as well as usual, setting up several useful attacks.

It was not until the second half that the Grecians added power to their finishing, which won them the game.

Alan Banks equalised with a good first time shot and six minutes later he grabbed another goal pouncing on a poor back pass.

In the last 15 minutes City had to defend in numbers as York tried almost desperate efforts, but with Keith Harvey holding the defence together, and he was absolutely brilliant, Exeter weathered the storm.

This was once again an excellent team performance and deserved a lot of praise as Exeter City moved into second place in the table.

WESTERN LEAGUE
Exeter City 1 Minehead 1
Scorers: Exeter City: Redwood.
Exeter City team: Parkhill, Quarrington, Arbury, Rutley, Henderson, Gough, Welsh, Redwood, Riding, Edgar, Spiers.

CITY SEARCH FOR TRAINING FACILITIES
Exeter City directors are looking for a 15-acre site as near as possible to the city centre which they can buy and develop for practice pitches and training facilities for the club.

Chairman Reg Rose has been looking privately for some time, but has been unable to find anything suitable and so the club has started advertising for land.

Rose said it was all part of the expansion programme which the Board has in mind for the club.

They have been badly needing extra training facilities for some time and this would provide the answer.

They would have pitches which they would be able to use for practice matches at almost any time when the St James' Park surface was unfit.

There would be proper sprint stretches and lapping circuits and a permanent circuit training course as well.

It would also mean that City no longer had to rent a separate pitch for the Colts side for their Exeter and District League games.

If possible a gymnasium would be erected so that the payers can have training facilities indoors in bad weather.

A gym has been needed for years, but it has never been possible because of the lack of space at St James' Park.

Monday 2nd March 1964

TORQUAY MATCH IS ALL TICKET
The Exeter City directors have decided that the Devon derby game against fellow promotion chasers Torquay United at St James' Park on Good Friday will be an all ticket match.

This will be a vital clash for both clubs and an attendance of around 15,000 is expected.

It has been decided to make it all ticket to avoid any delays at the turnstiles on the day of the game.

NEW FLOODLIGHTS
The board of directors have announced that they will not be trying out the new St James' Park floodlights at the City reserves versus Bristol City reserves Western League fixture on Wednesday night.

Originally they were going to use the game as an experiment, but they have decided that to bunch the new lights in one place would be unfair to the players, and to spread them around the ground would be an unfair test for the lights.

Tuesday 3rd March 1964

CITY FULL BACK SIDELINED FOR REST OF SEASON
Exeter City full back Roy Patrick will probably not be able to play again this season because of his back trouble.

At the moment he is in a plaster jacket and has been ordered to rest for at least six or seven weeks.

Patrick injured his back against Lincoln City in the first home match of the season.

He has tried to make a playing comeback on several occasions, but has been hit with a recurrence of the back injury caused by pressure on the sciatic nerve.

Wednesday 4th March 1964

Western League
Exeter City 0 Bristol City 4
Exeter City team: Parkhill, Quarrington, Parsons, Rutley, Henderson, Gough, Riding, Symington, Curtis, Edgar, Welsh.

ANOTHER CITY PLAYER TRANSFER LISTED
Young Irishman George Spiers has become the second player within a week to request a transfer from Exeter City.

He joins Scottish forward John Henderson in a bid to establish a first team place with another club.

Spiers, a tough 22-year-old, was signed from Crusaders two days before the season began,

He has made four appearances for City and wants to stay in the Football League rather than return to Ireland.

Thursday 5th March 1964

HENDERSON FOR CHELTENHAM?
Cheltenham Town have made an offer to sign Exeter City transfer listed forward, John Henderson.

Discussions are ongoing but City have told Cheltenham that they require an initial fee of £750, plus a further £250 by the 2nd May 1964.

Exeter also want 50 per cent of any transfer fee should Cheltenham sell the player to another club in the future

It is understood, however, that Henderson is not keen on the move and cannot agree terms with Cheltenham.

TRAINING FACILITIES: TWO POSSIBILITIES
Exeter City chairman Reg Rose will tell tonight's board meeting that there have been so far two replies to the club's advertisement for 15-acres of ground in or near the city to be used for training and practice.

So far though he has given no indication where the land is or whether it is suitable for City's use.

Friday 6th March 1964

FOURTH DIVISION TABLE

	P	W	D	L	F	A	Pts
Gillingham	34	17	11	6	45	21	45
Carlisle United	34	18	7	9	84	45	43
EXETER CITY	35	15	13	7	43	28	43
Workington	35	16	9	10	59	49	41
Torquay United	34	17	6	11	67	47	40
Bradford City	34	18	4	10	53	40	40
Brighton & H.A.	36	14	11	11	57	40	39
Lincoln City	34	15	9	10	53	51	39
Chester	34	16	6	12	53	44	38
Tranmere Rovers	34	13	11	10	61	53	37
Aldershot	34	14	6	14	67	65	34
Stockport County	35	12	10	13	41	50	34
Doncaster Rovers	34	12	9	13	57	55	33
Oxford United	32	12	8	12	45	43	32
Newport County	33	13	6	14	47	53	32
Darlington	35	10	11	14	48	73	31
Rochdale	32	10	10	12	42	37	30
Bradford P.A.	35	12	6	17	55	66	30
Chesterfield	32	11	7	14	40	51	29
Southport	34	11	7	16	50	67	29
Halifax Town	33	8	12	13	52	61	28
York City	34	9	5	20	37	50	23
Barrow	32	4	13	15	39	64	21
Hartlepools United	33	8	5	20	35	69	21

WESTERN LEAGUE TABLE

	P	W	D	L	F	A	Pts
Bridgwater Town	27	21	3	3	59	17	45
Bideford	29	19	5	5	73	31	43
Bristol City	27	16	10	1	77	26	42
Barnstaple Town	30	16	6	8	73	42	38
Andover	29	13	8	8	67	47	34
Torquay United	31	14	5	12	66	51	33
Yeovil Town	31	13	7	11	56	73	33
Dorchester Town	26	12	8	6	58	35	32
Welton Rovers	28	14	4	10	47	39	32
Weymouth	30	10	11	9	68	58	31
Salisbury City	28	13	5	10	53	46	31
Minehead	26	13	3	10	56	59	29
Bath City	29	9	9	11	58	67	27
Chippenham Town	29	10	4	15	48	41	24
Weston-Super-Mare	29	9	6	14	42	53	24
EXETER CITY	32	7	10	15	59	80	24
Poole Town	33	9	6	18	46	70	24
Frome Town	29	8	5	16	48	75	21
Glastonbury	29	7	5	17	51	72	19
Taunton Town	30	6	6	18	24	78	18
Portland United	28	7	3	18	49	84	17
Bridport	26	4	7	15	27	61	15

Your Goal after the Match

The GEORGE & DRAGON BLACKBOY ROAD

BASS ON DRAUGHT   GEORGE F. MILFORD, Proprietor   CITY ALES & STOUTS

Most of the nationally known bottled beers stocked

NORRINGTON'S of EXETER

Tel. 75315   For POWER FARMING EQUIPMENT of all kinds
ANY MAKE SUPPLIED   Largest Stock of Spares in the West

They do not want land which has already been scheduled for building upon as the price would be prohibitive.

Saturday 7th March 1964

Football League Game 36
Saturday March 7th
St James Park
5891

Exeter City	0 v 0	Barrow
Barnett	1	Caine
Smyth	2	Arrowsmith
MacDonald	3	Cahill
Mitchell	4	Eddy
Harvey	5	Wearmouth
Anderson	6	Clark
Rees	7	Maddison
Banks	8	Darwin
Thorne	9	Ackerley
Grace	10	Brennan
Ley	11	O'Neill

BARROVIANS PROVE TO BE HARD NUT TO CRACK

Exeter City had a point lopped off their promotion chances by being held to a draw by Barrow at St James' Park.

The visitors set out their stall right from kick off to play a defensive game, similar to that employed by City on their own away travels.

It was a case of Exeter being caught in their own trap. Barrow formed a solid defensive wall across the penalty area and City could not find a way through.

Everyone except Alan Barnett was in the Barrow half of the field at times, but despite all that attacking, and they must have had 90 per cent of the game, and all the threshing about in the penalty area, City had few chances to score.

Alan Banks did head the ball into the net as early as the very first minute, but he was ruled offside.

Barrow kept a tight rein on Banks and Adrian Thorne, and apart from Arnold Mitchell, no one else looked like doing anything.

If City had grabbed a couple of goals, supporters would have gone away praising a great display, instead of moaning at the loss of a point.

For almost all the football came from Exeter and in defence and midfield they moved very smoothly at times.

WESTERN LEAGUE
Poole Town 0 Exeter City 4
Scorers: Exeter City: Riding 3, Welsh.
Poole Town team: Linton, Leather, Drummond, McNeish, Penzer, Rushworth, Bodger, Robertson, McDowell, Hale, Brewster.

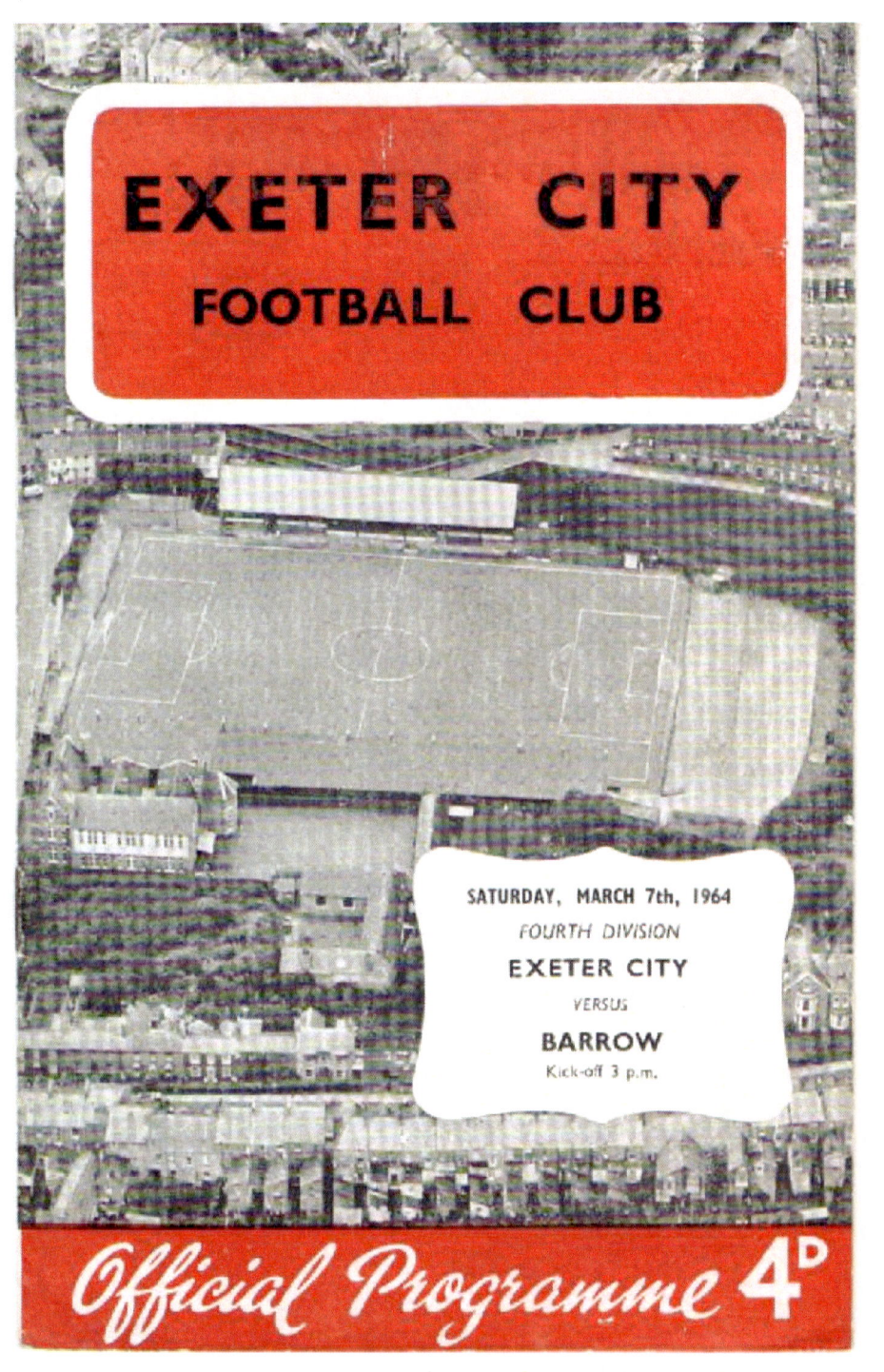

EXETER CITY FOOTBALL CLUB

SATURDAY, MARCH 7th, 1964

FOURTH DIVISION

EXETER CITY

VERSUS

BARROW

Kick-off 3 p.m.

Official Programme **4**ᴰ

The New Switchable Sheerline 8

Rediffusion's elegant new 19" Sheerline 8 is fully switchable to 625-line programmes. No aerials needed. Specially designed for Rediffusion's own wired television system, this set costs only £49. Rental £5 4s. Initial payment and 7s. 6d. a week reducing after minimum 1 year rental period. You simply switch on to enjoy a perfect picture free from fading or local interference.

PRESENT PROGRAMME SERVICE

TWW, Westward, BBC TV plus 3 radio programmes (including Luxembourg) all from one set for only 4/3 a week.

5 COLOUR FACIAS

Sheerline 8 is supplied with standard ocean green facia, or for 10/- extra choose from 4 other colours.

PART EXCHANGE

Your old set taken in part exchange when you buy or rent a new Sheerline 8.

MAINTENANCE SERVICE

Operates up to 10.00 p.m. every day, including Bank Holidays.

Regional Office:

BROAD PLAIN, BRISTOL 2

Tel.: Bristol 23332

Showrooms at:
Bristol: 6 Merchant Street, 1. Tel.: 23332.
Exeter: 149 Sidwell Street. Tel.: 76444.
Exmouth: 14 Victoria Road. Tel.: 3428.
Paignton: 50 Torquay Road. Tel.: 56321.
Penzance: 23/24 Market Place. Tel.: 2961.
Plymouth: 56 Cornwall St., or 8 Sawrey St. Tel.: 64071.
Southampton: 6 London Road, or 24/26 Lyon St., Tel.: 25321

OVER TO 625 L

EXETER CITY (o)o

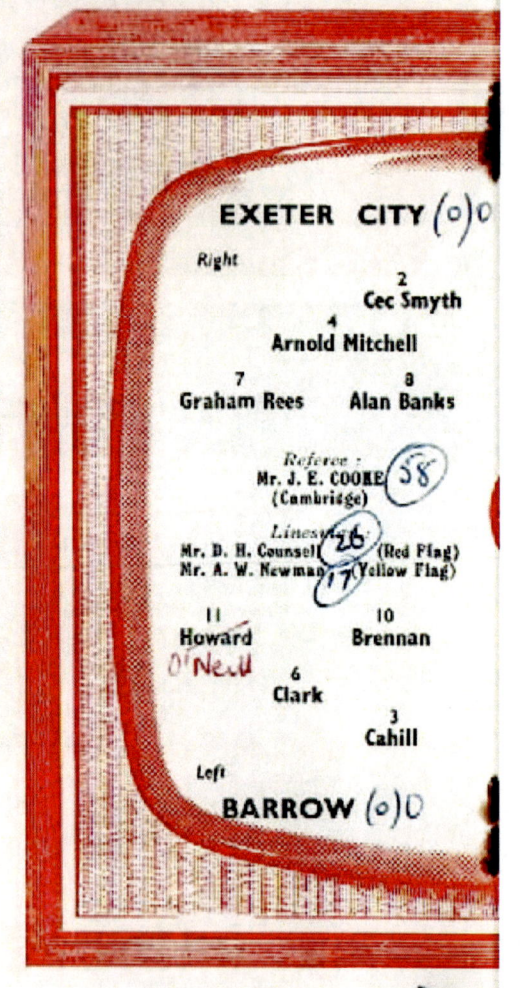

Right

2
Cec Smyth

4
Arnold Mitchell

7   8
Graham Rees   Alan Banks

Referee:
Mr. J. E. COOKE 58
(Cambridge)

Linesmen 26
Mr. D. H. Counsell (Red Flag)
Mr. A. W. Newman (Yellow Flag)

11   10
Howard   Brennan
O'Neill
                6
             Clark
                         3
                      Cahill

Left

BARROW (o)0

GET SET FOR 625 WITH T

INES — NO TROUBLE AT ALL

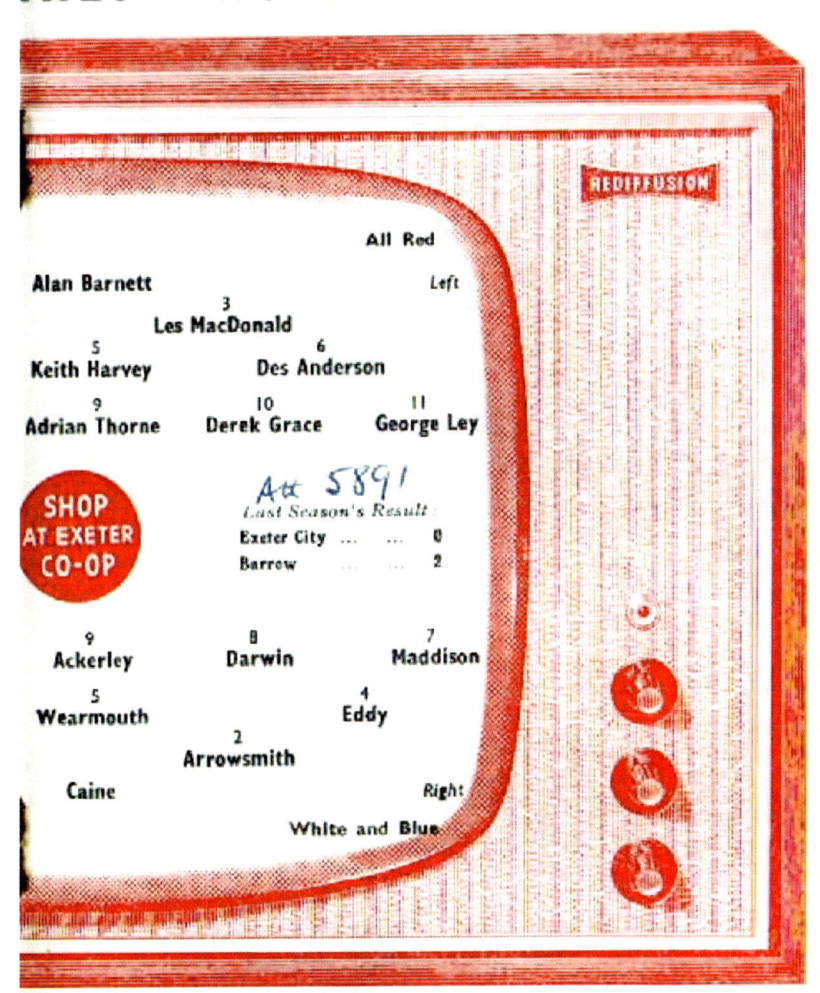

All Red
Left

Alan Barnett
3
Les MacDonald
5   6
Keith Harvey   Des Anderson
9   10   11
Adrian Thorne   Derek Grace   George Ley

Att 5891
Last Season's Result:
Exeter City   0
Barrow   2

SHOP AT EXETER CO-OP

9   8   7
Ackerley   Darwin   Maddison
5   4
Wearmouth   Eddy
           2
           Arrowsmith
Caine   Right
           White and Blue

REDIFFUSION

THE WIRED VISION SERVICE

Exeter City team: Parkhill, Quarrington, Parsons, Spiers, Henderson, Rutley, Welsh, Riding, Curtis, Gough, Symington.

Wednesday 11th March 1964

Western League
Exeter City 1 Dorchester Town 1
Scorers: Exeter City: Curtis.
Exeter City team: Parkhill, Quarrington, Parsons, Spiers, Henderson, Rutley, Welsh, Riding, Curtis, Gough, Edgar.

Friday 13th March 1964

CITY MAKE A BID FOR HANCOCK

Exeter City are attempting to sign another forward before the transfer deadline next Tuesday.

They would like to sign Exeter-born wing half and inside forward, Dave Hancock, who is playing for Devon rivals, Torquay United.

Hancock, who has been on the Torquay United transfer list at a fee of £1,500 would like to move to St James' Park, but United have said they won't give City an answer until Monday.

Saturday 14th March 1964

Football League Game 37
Saturday March 14th
Spotland
2113

Rochdale	1 v 3	Exeter City
Burgin	1	Barnett
Milburn	2	Smyth
Martin	3	MacDonald
Taylor	4	Grace
Aspden	5	Harvey
Thompson	6	Anderson
Wragg	7	Rees
Mckenzie	8	Banks(1)
Richardson	9	Curtis
Morton	10	Henderson
Storf	11	Thorne(2)

HIT AND RUN CITY

Mud and luck, both in very large lumps seem to be the generally accepted reasons for Exeter City's win over Rochdale.

Everyone in the side fought from start to finish. If they had not, if only one or two men had eased off, then Rochdale would have slaughtered them.

For the Dale had 80 per cent of the game, and any weakness in the City side would have given them the gap that they tried hard to find.

Exeter were quite content to let Rochdale make most of the running while they waited for a chance to strike. They scored three times using this ploy.

Alan Banks, at his hard grafting, goal grabbing best, got the first in the 19th minute and made another for Adrian Thorne shortly afterwards.

Then after Morton's 54th minute header had looked like putting Rochdale back in the game, Thorne got City's third.

City had slices of luck. Alan Barnett made two magnificent saves and City had to defend desperately at the end in the mud.

Rochdale were awarded a penalty which Milburn sliced yards wide as the rain lashed down.

Indeed there was a danger that the game may have been abandoned at one stage with the ball sometimes actually floating along in pools of water on the pitch.

WESTERN LEAGUE
Exeter City 2 Andover 2
Scorers: Exeter City: Redwood, Riding.
Exeter City team: Parkhill, Quarrington, Parker, Pope, Parsons, Rutley, Symington, Redwood, Riding, Welsh Spiers.
Andover: Morris, Voysey, Scurr, Heagren, Stevens, Primsall, Randell, Woolford, Hall, Case, Allen.

Exeter City included a 17-year old trialist, Terry Parker, at left back in the game against Andover. Parker came from Plymouth.

Monday 16th March 1964

STEVENS NOT FOR CITY
Swindon Town's 20-year-old centre forward, John Stevens, will not be joining Exeter City, despite being watched by club director Les Kerslake and City captain Arnold Mitchell on Saturday, when he scored two goals in a reserve game. However, the Grecians will watch Stevens again and he may be a target for next season.

SCOTTISH FORWARD FOR CITY
There will definitely be one new face at St James' Park tomorrow on transfer deadline day.   He is 20-year-old Scottish forward Walter Gerrard, who is with Glasgow Juvenile side Possil YM.   He will be having a one week trial with the Grecians.   Earlier in his career he had a spell on Brighton's books.

Tuesday 17th March 1964

HANCOCK SIGNS JUST IN TIME
Exeter City manager Jack Edwards and secretary Keith Honey made a late dash to Torquay last night to sign United's wing-half Dave Hancock for a fee of £1,000,

payable in two £500 instalments.

They beat the transfer deadline by just 15 minutes. Negotiations between the two clubs had twice broken down.

Yesterday afternoon City decided they would not pay Torquay the fee they wanted for the player. Edwards, however, changed his mind and moved quickly to sign Hancock.

Born in Exeter, Hancock started his professional career with Plymouth Argyle and was then loaned to Gillingham for a month before being transferred to Torquay United in December 1958.

He has played in more than 160 league matches for Torquay and had two previous transfer requests turned down by the Plainmoor club.

His latest came after being dropped from the side before Christmas and he has since been unable to regain his place.

Thursday 19th March 1964

HENDERSON CHANGES MIND ABOUT A TRANSFER
Exeter City inside forward John Henderson went on the transfer list at his own request last month, but he has now changed his mind.

No Football League clubs made approaches for him by the time the transfer deadline closed at midnight on Monday, so he asked the board to be removed from the transfer list and they agreed.

Henderson did receive one offer, but that was from a Southern League club, Cheltenham Town, which he turned down, as he wanted to stay in the Football League.

Saturday 21st March 1964

TEAM EFFORT THE WINNING WAY

Exeter City slogged in the mud to get two more points towards their promotion target of 58, which the club feel will be sufficient.

For only a wholehearted effort from everyone in the side got them the win over Oxford United, a team which had a tough defence and a waspishly determined forward line.

From Alan Barnett to Adrian Thorne, the players worked so hard in the muddy conditions, as they showed fight and persistence. It was a great team effort.

Oxford took the lead n the 20th minute when Calder whipped in a Quartermain free kick past a static City defence.

Friday 20th March 1964

FOURTH DIVISION TABLE

	P	W	D	L	F	A	Pts
Gillingham	35	18	11	6	47	22	47
EXETER CITY	37	16	14	7	46	29	46
Carlisle United	37	19	8	10	90	49	46
Workington	37	18	9	10	64	49	45
Bradford City	37	20	5	12	58	53	45
Torquay United	35	18	6	11	71	45	42
Brighton & H.A.	38	15	11	12	60	42	41
Chester	38	17	6	15	58	50	40
Tranmere Rovers	36	14	11	11	63	55	39
Lincoln City	36	15	9	12	54	56	39
Aldershot	37	15	7	15	70	69	37
Halifax Town	37	12	12	13	62	66	36
Oxford United	35	13	9	13	51	48	36
Doncaster Rovers	36	12	10	14	59	58	34
Stockport County	37	12	10	15	42	56	34
Rochdale	36	11	11	14	47	44	33
Chesterfield	35	13	7	15	46	54	33
Darlington	37	11	11	15	51	76	33
Newport County	35	13	6	16	47	57	32
Southport	36	12	7	17	53	71	31
Bradford P.A.	36	12	6	18	55	70	30
York City	35	10	5	20	40	50	25
Barrow	35	4	15	16	42	69	23
Hartlepools United	35	8	6	21	37	75	22

WESTERN LEAGUE TABLE

	P	W	D	L	F	A	Pts
Bridgwater Town	30	23	3	4	64	19	49
Bristol City	30	19	10	1	92	26	48
Bideford	31	21	5	5	76	32	47
Barnstaple Town	33	18	6	9	77	46	42
Dorchester Town	29	14	9	6	68	38	37
Torquay United	33	16	5	12	71	53	37
Andover	32	13	9	10	69	54	35
Weymouth	32	12	11	9	73	59	35
Yeovil Town	35	14	7	12	62	76	35
Welton Rovers	28	14	4	10	47	39	32
Salisbury City	30	13	6	11	54	48	32
Minehead	28	13	4	11	58	62	30
Bath City	31	9	10	12	60	71	28
EXETER CITY	36	8	12	16	66	87	28
Chippenham Town	31	10	5	16	49	43	25
Weston-Super-Mare	31	9	7	15	43	59	25
Poole Town	35	9	6	20	46	77	24
Taunton Town	33	8	6	19	29	81	22
Frome Town	31	8	5	18	50	80	21
Glastonbury	31	7	5	19	51	76	19
Portland United	30	8	3	19	51	89	19
Bridport	28	4	8	16	27	68	16

THE GRECIANS' ASSOCIATION present

BINGO

Commencing 7.30 p.m.

on the following MONDAYS:

Mar. 2nd, 9th, 16th, 23rd & 30th

CIVIC HALL   Admission 2/6 (including playing tickets)

BARTLETT & SON (EXETER) LTD.

Directors: R. A. CRAGG   M. G. CRAGG

PRINTERS for ALL SPORTING OCCASIONS

138, COWICK STREET
EXETER

Telephone 54086

Football League Game 38
Saturday March 21st
St James Park
6602

Exeter City	3 v 2	Oxford United
Barnett	1	Rouse
Smyth	2	Beavon
MacDonald	3	Quartermain
Grace	4	Atkinson
Harvey	5	Kyle
Anderson	6	Jones
Rees	7	Knight
Banks	8	Longbottom(1)
Curtis(1)	9	Calder(1)
Hancock	10	Hartland
Thorne(1)	11	Harrington
(Kyle(og))		

Ten minutes later the Grecians were back on terms when Adrian Thorne headed home a cross from Dermot Curtis.

In the 36th minute Curtis himself scored, after taking a pass from Derek Grace, beating one man and shooting past keeper Rouse.

Seven minutes before half time it was all square again when Longbottom shot through a crowd of players.

City may have been a little fortunate with the winning goal in the 76th minute when Kyle deflected a Graham Rees cross into his own net, but they had done enough to deserve it.

For every attempt Oxford had, City had three. Dave Hancock gave a competent, hard working performance on his debut.

CITY SNIPPETS
Exeter City need only two away points to equal the club's record away bag of 22 points in a season which was the total netted in the 1932-33 campaign when they finished as runners-up in the Third Division South, and equalled in 1953-54 when the Grecians were ninth. Exeter currently have the best away record in the Fourth Division and there are only five clubs in the entire Football League with a better away total.

Derby games are often exciting, but never has so much depended on the results of the meetings between Exeter City and Torquay United, for with both clubs well up in the promotion race, a 'double' for either side could see that club through to the Third Division, while it would almost certainly put paid to the defeated club's promotion hopes.

Good Friday 27th March 1964

ALL SQUARE IN THE DEVON DERBY

This was a very good result for Torquay United and they worked hard to get it, but they were lucky to get away with it.

Three times Exeter City had the ball n the net. Once Dermot Curtis was plainly offside. Once Arnold Mitchell even more plainly handled in a Graham Rees cross.

Thursday 26th March 1964

FOURTH DIVISION TABLE

	P	W	D	L	F	A	Pts
Carlisle United	38	20	8	10	96	49	48
EXETER CITY	38	17	14	7	49	31	48
Gillingham	35	18	11	6	47	22	47
Workington	38	19	9	10	66	50	47
Bradford City	38	20	6	12	59	54	46
Torquay United	36	18	7	11	72	46	43
Brighton & H.A.	39	15	11	13	60	43	41
Tranmere Rovers	37	15	11	13	67	57	41
Chester	39	17	7	15	59	51	41
Lincoln City	37	16	9	12	57	58	41
Aldershot	38	16	7	15	71	69	39
Halifax Town	38	13	12	13	64	67	38
Oxford United	36	13	9	14	53	51	35
Doncaster Rovers	37	12	10	15	59	64	34
Chesterfield	36	13	8	15	47	55	34
Stockport County	38	12	10	16	44	60	34
Rochdale	37	11	11	15	48	46	33
Southport	37	13	7	17	55	72	33
Darlington	37	11	11	15	51	76	33
Newport County	35	13	6	16	47	57	32
Bradford P.A.	37	12	6	19	56	72	30
York City	36	10	5	21	42	53	25
Barrow	35	4	15	16	42	69	23
Hartlepools United	36	8	6	22	36	77	22

WESTERN LEAGUE TABLE

	P	W	D	L	F	A	Pts
Bristol City	32	21	10	1	99	26	52
Bridgwater Town	32	23	4	5	67	24	50
Bideford	32	22	5	5	79	33	49
Barnstaple Town	33	18	6	9	77	46	42
Dorchester Town	30	14	10	6	68	38	38
Andover	33	14	9	10	72	56	37
Torquay United	35	16	5	14	72	57	37
Yeovil Town	34	15	7	12	64	77	37
Weymouth	33	12	11	10	74	62	35
Welton Rovers	29	15	4	10	50	40	34
Salisbury City	30	13	6	11	54	48	32
Minehead	30	13	5	12	62	67	31
Bath City	32	9	10	13	60	72	28
EXETER CITY	36	8	12	16	66	87	28
Chippenham Town	32	11	5	16	51	43	27
Weston-Super-Mare	32	10	7	15	48	59	27
Poole Town	36	10	6	20	49	77	26
Frome Town	32	8	6	18	50	80	22
Taunton Town	34	8	6	20	30	85	22
Glastonbury	32	8	5	19	55	77	21
Portland United	31	8	3	20	51	92	19
Bridport	30	4	8	18	27	78	16

Clock Tower Cafe
(EXETER) LTD.
Exeter's Leading and Largest
EXPRESSO COFFEE BAR (Seating 150)

2-COURSE Luncheons 4/-
12 noon—2 p.m.
Phone 72119
Open until 11 p.m. nightly

Austins
Telephone 75815
FOR OUTSIDE CATERING
68 Bartholomew Street West, Exeter
Official Caterers to Exeter City F.C.

Football League Game 39
Friday March 27th
St James Park
16141

Exeter City	0 v 0	Torquay United
Barnett	1	Adlington
Smyth	2	Williams
MacDonald	3	Allen
Hancock	4	Spencer
Harvey	5	Bettany
Anderson	6	Wolstenholme
Rees	7	Anderson
Banks	8	Northcott
Curtis	9	Handley
Mitchell	10	Jenkins
Thorne	11	Pym

But between those in the 30th minute, a Curtis goal was disallowed for offside only after the referee changed his mind after consultation with a linesman.

Alan Banks was the terror of the Torquay defence and made several worthwhile efforts. There were also several moments of panic for United as City milled around in their goal mouth.

Obviously City made mistakes. It was a typical, scrappy derby match that was full of petty fouls and misdemeanours. The City have played better and lost.

The Grecians' defence made nonsense of the much feared Torquay attack. Dave Hancock completely bottled up Jenkins, but it was Des Anderson who was the outstanding defender.

Anderson got through a tremendous amount of work and covered everyone so well, Everything points to cracking game in the return meeting between the two clubs on Monday.

WESTERN LEAGUE
Bideford 2 Exeter City 0
Exeter City team: Parkhill, Quarrington, Gillard, Spiers, Parsons, Gough, Welsh, Gerrard, Gifford, Rutley, Ley.

Saturday 28th March 1964

Western League
Exeter City 2 Frome Town 2
Scorers: Exeter City: Gerrard, Ley.
Exeter City team: Parkhill, Quarrington, Arbury, Pope, Henderson, Rutley, Welsh, Riding, Gerrard, Redwood, Ley.

Easter Monday 30th March 1964

Football League Game 40
Monday March 30th
Plainmoor
13655

Torquay United	1 v 1	Exeter City
Adlington	1	Barnett
Williams	2	Smyth
Allen	3	MacDonald
Spencer	4	Hancock
Bettany	5	Harvey
Wolstenholme	6	Anderson
Anderson	7	Rees
Stubbs	8	Banks
Handley(1)	9	Curtis(1)
Jenkins	10	Grace
Pym	11	Thorne

CITY KEEP IN THE RUNNING FOR PROMOTION

The teams stumbled through this match, so anxious not to lose. Neither of these promotion contenders could afford to lose.

Alan Banks was again Exeter City's most dangerous forward, and it was from his cross in the 14th minute that Dermot Curtis dived full length to head past Adlington to put the Grecians ahead.

Torquay were persistent though and in the 28th minute were back on terms when Handley fired into the net.

Pym scrambled the ball into goal, but it was disallowed for handball as City were forced back on the defensive for long spells.

When they did move forward City lost the ball all too often in the midfield area so their attacks broke down, before they really got started.

They did have a good spell midway through the half though, and Dave Hancock had a drive well saved by Adlington.

The game fell away into a final scrappy 20 minutes as both teams seemed content with the draw.

There is no doubt, like so many matches this season, that it was dominated by City's defence.

Two points from the Easter games keeps City well in the running for promotion, but the team's main failing was not being able to switch quickly enough from defence to attack.

WESTERN LEAGUE
Exeter City 0 Bideford 2

TORQUAY UNITED A.F.C.
Official Programme

TORQUAY from CORBYN HEAD — Photo by permission of Torquay Publicity Committee

TORQUAY UNITED
v.
EXETER CITY
MONDAY, 30th MARCH, 1964
Kick-off 10.30 a.m.

SIXPENCE

3944

Friday 3rd April 1964

FOURTH DIVISION TABLE

	P	W	D	L	F	A	Pts
Carlisle United	41	21	9	11	102	55	51
Gillingham	38	21	12	7	50	25	50
EXETER CITY	40	17	16	7	50	31	50
Workington	41	20	10	11	68	52	50
Bradford City	41	22	6	13	65	56	50
Torquay United	38	18	9	11	84	47	45
Tranmere Rovers	41	17	11	13	76	65	45
Brighton & H.A.	41	16	12	13	63	44	44
Halifax Town	41	15	13	13	72	70	43
Chester	42	17	8	17	60	55	42
Aldershot	41	16	9	16	73	73	41
Lincoln City	40	16	9	15	60	68	41
Chesterfield	39	14	10	15	50	77	38
Stockport County	41	14	10	17	48	63	38
Doncaster Rovers	40	13	12	15	65	68	38
Oxford United	39	13	11	15	55	54	37
Darlington	40	13	11	16	59	82	37
Newport County	39	15	6	18	55	64	36
Rochdale	40	11	13	16	51	51	35
Bradford P.A.	40	14	7	19	61	73	35
Southport	40	14	7	19	60	80	35
York City	39	11	6	22	45	57	28
Hartlepools United	40	9	8	23	45	86	26
Barrow	38	4	17	17	66	73	25

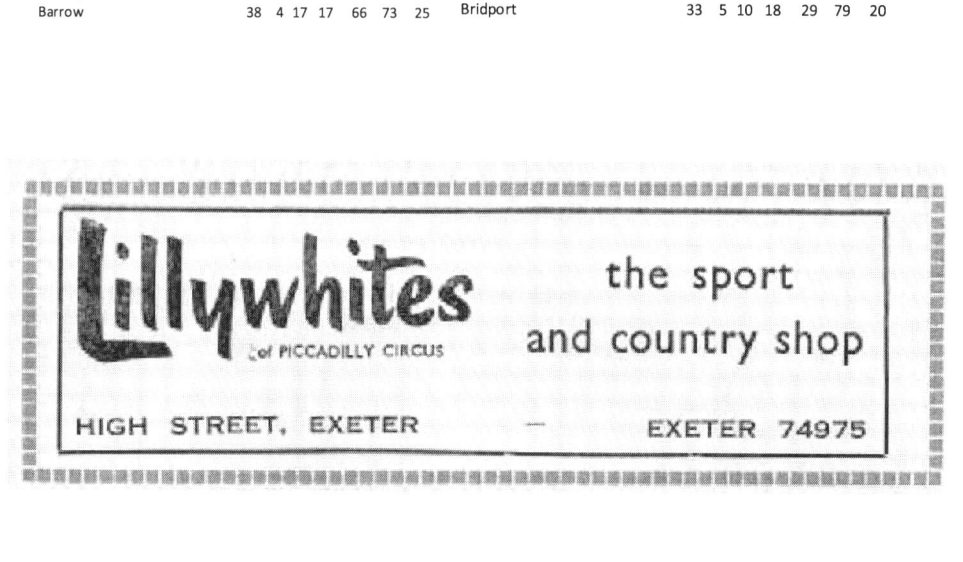

WESTERN LEAGUE TABLE

	P	W	D	L	F	A	Pts
Bristol City	35	22	11	2	103	31	55
Bideford	35	25	5	5	86	33	55
Bridgwater Town	35	23	7	5	68	25	53
Barnstaple Town	36	18	8	8	80	50	44
Dorchester Town	33	14	13	6	70	40	41
Yeovil Town	37	16	8	13	67	80	40
Welton Rovers	32	17	5	10	57	42	39
Weymouth	36	14	11	11	86	66	39
Andover	36	15	9	12	76	61	39
Torquay United	36	16	5	15	72	60	37
Salisbury City	33	15	6	12	60	52	36
Minehead	33	15	6	12	73	70	36
Chippenham Town	35	13	5	17	58	48	31
Bath City	35	9	11	15	64	80	29
Weston-Super-Mare	35	10	9	16	51	68	29
EXETER CITY	39	8	13	18	68	93	29
Poole Town	38	11	6	21	52	80	28
Frome Town	35	9	7	19	55	85	25
Taunton Town	36	8	8	20	32	87	24
Glastonbury	35	9	5	21	58	82	23
Portland United	34	8	4	22	53	106	20
Bridport	33	5	10	18	29	79	20

Lillywhites of PICCADILLY CIRCUS — the sport and country shop

HIGH STREET, EXETER — EXETER 74975

Exeter City team: Parkhill, Quarrington, Edmunds, Pope, Henderson, Rutley, Welsh, Riding, Gerrard, Redwood, Ley.

Saturday 4th April 1964

Football League Game 41
Saturday April 4th
St James Park
6077

Exeter City	3 v 1	Newport County
Parkhill	1	Weare
Smyth	2	Frowen
MacDonald	3	Walters
Hancock	4	Rowland
Harvey(1)	5	Rathbone
Anderson	6	Hill
Rees	7	Smith
Banks(2)	8	Sheffield
Curtis	9	Reynolds(1)
Grace	10	Hunt
Thorne	11	Pring

CITY MADE IT HARD WORK

Exeter City may have gained two more points toward their promotion push, but it was not that comfortably achieved, despite the score line which suggests otherwise.

City made it very hard going for themselves, for they should have made mincemeat of a Newport County side that was ragged in defence and weak in the forward line.

The Grecians, however, missed chance after chance. Some of Exeter's attacks foundered because of bad finishing, some because of brilliant goalkeeping by Weare, and some because of over elaboration.

Once again most of the work in the forward line fell on Alan Banks and once again he scored one of his typical goals, darting through the Newport defence to net after 31 minutes.

Then after Keith Harvey had scored from the penalty spot, and Reynolds hit an 80th minute drive past Jimmy Parkhill, Banks bobbed up again to make sure of the win for Exeter with another good goal.

The tension in the City team at this crucial stage of the promotion race showed. No one can blame them for wanting to play it safe, but they do rely heavily on their defence at times.

Keith Harvey was once again outstanding, whilst debutant goalkeeper, Parkhill, who has waited for his chance all season in the City reserves, produced a sound display.

WESTERN LEAGUE
Welton Rovers 3 Exeter City 1
Scorers: Welton Rovers: Boxley 2, Simmons. Exeter City: Redwood.
Exeter City team: Thompson, Quarrington, Edmunds, Rutley, Henderson, Gough, Welsh, Redwood, Riding, Edgar, Ley.

Wednesday 6th April 1964

RIDING OFFERED PART TIME TERMS
Exeter City are to offer forward Alan Riding a part-time professional contract to commence as form next season.

Riding, who is a regular in the City reserve side, works for Exeter City Council, and the contract will be subject to them agreeing to allowing the player time off when required for travelling to matches.

Saturday 11th April 1964

STALEMATE AT COUNTY

Football League Game 42
Saturday April 11th
Edgeley Park
2773

Stockport County	0 v 0	Exeter City
Beighton	1	Barnett
Johnston	2	Smyth
Cuthbert	3	MacDonald
Wylie	4	Hancock
Parry	5	Harvey
Ricketts	6	Anderson
Watt	7	Rees
Ryden	8	Banks
France	9	Curtis
Davenport	10	Grace
Davcock	11	Ley

Another game and another point towards promotion. there was nothing fine or fancy about it to praise and few things to draw any real criticism, just a hard afternoon's work.

It was a tough game, a hard ground and a gusty wind made conditions difficult.

Stockport County were content to use the long ball, while Exeter kept it close until they could make a final break.

Both teams also had blanket defences and so it did not work out too well for either of them.

There were some really breath holding moments in each goal and City had as much good luck as bad in some of these.

Then between the bright spots there was a nervousness about the play which prevented any kind of pattern being favoured or followed.

Often the City forward were just stopped by sheer defensive power which they could not do anything about.

Dermot Curtis had a goal disallowed for offside and saw another shot rebound from the post with Beighton beaten.

When Alan Banks is bottled up, that is the end of the City forward line and Stockport did just that.

Scrumptious — Mummy always uses

TOPZ SELF RAISING FLOUR

NELSTROPS Millers STOCKPORT

Stockport County
v.
Exeter C.

Saturday, 11th April, 1964

Kick-off 3—0 p.m.

FOOTBALL LEAGUE DIVISION FOUR

No. 2351

Official Programme : 6d

B. & T. BREWER & TURNBULL (GREENUP) LIMITED

32-40 LONDON ROAD, HAZEL GROVE, STOCKPORT
Tel.: STE 1424/8

Also at:
BLACKPOOL, BIRMINGHAM, BRIGHTON, GLASGOW, HARROGATE, LIVERPOOL & LONDON

REMOVALS · STORAGE
PACKING · SHIPPING

Quotations and Advice without obligation

Yet there were times when a little more imaginative thought and speed would have got them through the hosts rearguard.

WESTERN LEAGUE
Exeter City 3 Bath City 3
Scorers: Exeter City: Riding 2, Edgar.
Exeter City team: Parkhill, Quarrington, Gough, Rutley, Parsons, Spiers, Welsh, Dodd, Riding, Edgar, Ley.

Monday 13th April 1964

Football League Game 43
Monday April 13th
Saltergate
4442

Chesterfield	0 v 1	Exeter City
Powell	1	Barnett
Holmes	2	Smyth
Sears	3	MacDonald
Clarke	4	Hancock
Blakey	5	Harvey
Whitham	6	Anderson
Duncan	7	Rees
Frost	8	Banks(1)
Frear	9	Curtis
Rackstraw	10	Grace
Hughes	11	Ley

EXETER CITY: TOP OF THE TABLE

Exeter City's single goal victory over Chesterfield moved them up to the top of the Fourth Division for the first time this season.

They have now used their game in hand, but with three matches to go have a one point lead over Workington, Carlisle United and Bradford City.

After this win City vice chairman George Gillin joined the team in a special wine toast to celebrate City going to the top of the table, but it was a game won at a high price.

The game's outstanding defender, Keith Harvey, had to see the Chesterfield doctor after the match to stitch a cut above his eye, after being caught by an elbow in the last minute.

Alan Banks, City's lone goal hero, injured the muscles in his upper left arm, which had him playing most of the second half with his arm held to his side.

The only goal of the game came after 25 minutes when a break through engineered by Dermot Curtis and Graham Rees ended in Banks shooting past Powell from an acute angle.

Banks admitted afterwards that it had been an attempted centre for Adrian Thorne to run on to.

SEASON 1963-64

CHESTERFIELD FOOTBALL CLUB

Official Programme
Fourpence

Registered Office:
RECREATION GROUND
CHESTERFIELD

Telephone
2318

FOOTBALL LEAGUE — FOURTH DIVISION

Friday 17th April 1964

FOURTH DIVISION TABLE

	P	W	D	L	F	A	Pts
EXETER CITY	43	19	17	7	54	33	55
Gillingham	41	21	12	8	55	27	54
Carlisle United	43	22	10	11	15	56	54
Workington	43	22	12	7	72	52	54
Bradford City	43	24	6	13	74	58	54
Torquay United	42	20	9	13	78	50	49
Tranmere Rovers	43	19	11	13	80	67	49
Brighton & H.A.	43	17	12	14	66	47	46
Aldershot	43	18	9	16	80	75	45
Chester	44	18	8	18	63	59	44
Halifax Town	43	15	13	15	72	75	43
Lincoln City	42	17	9	16	62	70	43
Chesterfield	43	15	11	17	54	64	41
Oxford United	41	14	12	15	58	55	40
Doncaster Rovers	43	14	12	17	68	71	40
Newport County	42	16	7	19	60	68	39
Stockport County	43	14	11	18	48	66	39
Bradford P.A.	42	15	8	19	66	76	38
Darlington	43	13	12	18	63	89	38
Rochdale	43	11	14	18	53	56	36
Southport	43	14	8	21	61	87	36
York City	42	12	7	23	50	63	31
Hartlepools United	43	10	9	24	50	90	29
Barrow	42	5	17	20	47	85	27

WESTERN LEAGUE

	P	W	D	L	F	A	Pts
Bideford	38	26	6	6	93	35	58
Bridgwater Town	38	24	9	5	76	27	57
Bristol City	37	22	12	3	104	34	56
Welton Rovers	36	21	5	10	71	47	47
Dorchester Town	37	16	13	8	78	50	45
Barnstaple Town	38	18	9	11	85	58	45
Yeovil Town	39	17	8	14	70	88	42
Weymouth	39	15	11	13	92	70	41
Andover	38	16	9	13	79	68	41
Salisbury City	36	16	7	13	64	56	39
Torquay United	39	17	5	17	76	71	39
Minehead	37	16	7	14	78	76	39
Chippenham Town	38	15	6	17	70	54	36
Bath City	39	10	12	17	73	89	32
Weston-Super-Mare	38	11	10	17	55	73	32
EXETER CITY	41	8	14	19	72	99	30
Frome Town	38	10	9	19	59	87	29
Poole Town	39	11	6	22	54	83	28
Glastonbury	38	10	7	21	63	83	27
Portland United	38	10	5	23	60	112	25
Bridport	37	6	12	19	31	83	24
Taunton Town	38	8	8	22	32	92	24

---

for Structural Engineering and Heavy Platework

REDHEUGH-WILLEY Ltd

WATER LANE, EXETER

EXETER 74064 P.B.X.

Exeter had shown great determination and team work, with Harvey absolutely outstanding in City's defensive plan.

Friday 17th April 1964

PROMOTION RACE HOTS UP
Promotion is never easy. Exeter City have gone 12 games without defeat, yet even now, with only three more games to play, the Grecians are still not sure of breaking through to the Third Division.

There is no doubt that whoever makes it this time will certainly have earned promotion, for all six clubs left in the race are setting a hot pace.

Up until last Monday's games, City had lost once in 13 games, Carlisle United once in seven games, Bradford City once in nine, Gillingham once in three, Torquay United once in 11, and Workington once in eight games.

BANKS IS CITY SUPPORTERS' FAVOURITE
Despite the strain of the promotion race, one player is enjoying his football, perhaps more than any other.

Alan Banks has given performances that clearly give the impression that he really is bubbling over with enthusiasm.

The player had certainly won the hearts of City supporters in the comparatively short time that he has been with the club.

Banks has now netted 16 goals in 26 appearances ad one wonders just how many goals he would have got had he been with City from the start of the season.

Saturday 18th April 1964

Football League Game 44
Saturday April 18th
St James Park
9722

Exeter City	2 v 3	Bradford (Park Avenue)
Barnett	1	Hardie
Smyth	2	Thomas
MacDonald	3	Lightowler
Hancock	4	Atkinson
Harvey(1)	5	McCalman
Anderson	6	Flynn
Rees(1)	7	Lawrie(1)
Henderson	8	Hector(1)
Curtis	9	Fryatt
Grace	10	Spratt(1)
Thorne	11	Bird

PROMOTION SETBACK FOR THE GRECIANS

Bradford Park Avenue dealt a big blow to Exeter City's chances of playing in the Third Division next season, for the Grecians have a real uphill climb now with only one home game left.

They badly missed the dash and

opportunism of the injured Alan Banks. He would have snapped up the chances that went begging.

Dermot Curtis fought a lone battle, but his tireless energy could not inspire the rest of the team.

Exeter were so anxious to avoid mistakes or challenge that they let Bradford get away with too much.

It was this attitude that allowed Hector through in the 14th minute to equalise Keith Harvey's early penalty.

Graham Rees, the only real danger man in the Exeter attack, put them back in front with a 26th minute shot, but by half time City had thrown the lead away again when Spratt had scored.

The second half was even more disastrous for the Grecians. They struggled to contain Spratt and Hector and they gave away another goal to Lawrie in the 64th minute.

In fact they could have easily conceded two further goals had it not been for Alan Barnett making two good saves.

The 9,722 crowd left St James' Park thoroughly depressed wondering if this game had cost Exeter City promotion for the first time in their history.

Monday 20th April 1964

GRECIAN RECORD BREAKERS
The outstanding feature of Exeter City's play this season has not been in the goalscoring department, but in the defence, and here the Grecians owe a big vote of thanks to Keith Harvey and company for creating a new club record for the fewest number of goals conceded in a Football League season.

Indeed this could well be an all time club record since Exeter City turned professional in 1908, beating one which was set up in the Southern League days when in season 1913-14 City conceded only 38 goals.

It should be noted though that was in only 38 games played. At the moment City have only let in 36 goals in 44 games, so they can say even now that this has actually been the best ever by a City team.

Apart from the record number of away points which City have earned this season, there may also be two other records that will be equalled.

At the moment the Grecians have suffered only two home defeats and that equals the best in seasons 1931-32 and 1932-33. The record for the smallest number of away defeats is six in season 1932-33.

Monday 20th April 1964

FOURTH DIVISION TABLE

	P	W	D	L	F	A	Pts
Carlisle United	44	24	10	11	109	56	56
Workington	44	23	10	11	74	52	56
Bradford City	44	25	6	13	76	59	56
Gillingham	44	19	17	8	56	36	55
Exeter City	44	19	17	8	56	36	55
Torquay United	43	20	9	14	78	51	49
Tranmere Rovers	44	19	11	14	81	69	49
Brighton & H.A.	44	18	12	14	68	49	48
Aldershot	44	18	10	16	81	76	46
Halifax Town	44	16	13	15	73	75	45
Chester	45	18	8	19	63	60	44
Lincoln City	43	17	9	17	62	72	43
Chesterfield	44	15	11	18	54	63	41
Oxford United	43	14	12	17	59	59	40
Doncaster Rovers	44	14	12	18	68	73	40
Bradford P.A.	43	16	8	19	69	78	40
Darlington	44	14	12	18	65	89	40
Newport County	43	16	8	19	61	89	40
Stockport County	44	14	11	19	48	68	39
Southport	44	15	8	21	63	87	38
Rochdale	44	11	15	18	59	57	37
York City	43	13	7	23	51	63	33
Hartlepools United	44	11	9	24	51	90	31
Barrow	43	5	17	21	48	89	27

WESTERN LEAGUE TABLE

	P	W	D	L	F	A	Pts
Bideford	39	27	6	6	98	35	60
Bristol City	39	23	13	3	112	39	59
Bridgwater Town	38	24	9	5	76	27	57
Barnstaple Town	39	19	9	11	89	60	47
Welton Rovers	37	21	5	11	72	49	47
Dorchester Town	38	16	14	8	79	51	46
Andover	39	16	10	13	84	73	42
Yeovil Town	40	17	8	15	70	90	42
Weymouth	40	15	11	14	92	73	41
Salisbury City	37	17	7	13	66	57	41
Minehead	38	17	7	14	82	76	41
Torquay United	39	17	5	17	76	71	39
Chippenham Town	39	15	6	18	70	56	36
Bath City	40	11	12	17	75	89	34
Weston-Super-Mare	39	11	10	18	55	78	32
Frome Town	39	11	9	19	61	87	31
EXETER CITY	41	8	14	19	72	99	30
Poole Town	39	11	6	22	54	83	28
Glastonbury	39	10	7	22	64	87	27
Portland United	38	10	5	23	60	112	25
Bridport	38	6	13	19	32	84	25
Taunton Town	39	8	8	23	34	96	24

A win against Chesterfield tomorrow would also mean a post war record number of 'doubles' completed, for they have already bagged maximum points from Bradford City, Oxford United, Newport County and York City. Exeter haven't had as many 'doubles' in a season since 1932-33 when they chalked up six.

Tuesday 21st April 1964

THIS WAS CITY AT THEIR BEST

Football League Game 45
Tuesday April 21st
St James Park
9449

Exeter City	6 v 1	Chesterfield
Barnett	1	Powell
Smyth	2	Holmes
MacDonald	3	Poole
Hancock	4	Clarke
Harvey	5	Blakey
Anderson	6	Lovie
Rees(1)	7	Duncan
Banks(2)	8	Frost
Curtis(1)	9	Frear
Hancock	10	Hughes
Thorne(2)	11	Rackstraw(1)

It has been a very long time since a crowd stood to cheer an Exeter City team off the pitch at St James' Park, but they did so at the end of this game.

For the Grecians had displayed 90 minutes of furious, fighting football as they smashed their way to a resounding win over Chesterfield and a place back in the race to the Third Division.

Once again Alan Banks was the hero and their inspiration. It was magnificent stuff to watch and a carnival atmosphere to go with it.

City took the lead in the 27th minute when Graham Rees cracked in a low shot past Powell after receiving a pass from Dermot Curtis.

Eleven minutes later Curtis headed a Dave Hancock centre to Banks who made no mistake for goal number two.

At half time an impromptu game of football was played across the pitch by lads who had climbed over the railings, but no one bothered them, such was the relaxed atmosphere and they happily made their way back to the terraces when the players returned for the second half.

City picked up where they had left off and in the 52nd minute it was 3-0 as Curtis diverted a Rees centre into the net via a post.

Seven minutes later Banks ran through the centre of the Chesterfield defence to score from 18-yards, and in the 66th minute Banks pulled the ball back to Adrian Thorne to net the fifth goal with a thundering shot.

Ten minutes from the end Chesterfield had their one success of the evening when

Rackstraw scored from close in following a free kick.

Exeter scored their sixth and final goal in the 87th minute and again it was Thorne with a tremendous drive.

What a night this was! A night that will be savoured for a very long time. City will surely travel to Workington for their final match of the season in very good heart.

WHO ARE CITY'S FASTEST SCORERS?
Since signing for Exeter City, prior to the game against Chesterfield, Alan Banks had scored 16 goals in 26 appearances. Only five men in the club's history have scored goals at a faster rate:-

	Season	Goals	Appearances	Rate
Fred Whitlow	1932-33	34	33	1.030
Fred Goodwin	1914-15	23	26	0.884
Harold Blackmore	1926-27	25	33	0.757
Rod Williams	1936-37	29	41	0.707
Fred Dent	1927-28	25	34	0.705
Alan Banks	1963-64	16	26	0.615
Ted Calland	1958-59	27	44	0.613

Wednesday 22nd April 1964

CITY NEED A POINT FOR PROMOTION
One more point and Exeter City are sure of promotion for the first time in the club's history.

That is the position with just one game to go. City travel to Workington (who are in third place) this Saturday.

If Bradford City lose tonight and again at York City on Saturday, Exeter need no more points, so they could still lose at Workington and still be promoted on goal average.

The position at the top of the Fourth Division is so tight City must aim for at least one point to be absolutely certain on their last trip to the north this season.

Thursday 23rd April 1964

IT'S ALL IN THE MELTING POT!
Exeter City supporters who are anxiously summing up their teams chances of promotion have been split into two factions after Workington's win at Bradford City last night.

There are those who take it as a good omen because they say Workington will not be quite as desperate to win when they meet Exeter on Saturday in an all deciding game. One point apiece, they rightly point out will see each team promoted.

There are those who say that getting two points at Bradford City, will mean Workington will be full of confidence and go all out for two more on the off chance of winning the Fourth Division championship.

The position at the top of the Fourth Division is so tight that it is difficult to forecast anything except to say that with one point on Saturday, Exeter City must be promoted and that even if they are defeated, goal average would still put them up if Bradford City lose at York City.

All five Exeter City directors will travel to Workington on Saturday and British Railways have a special excursion fare offer for the match.

This should mean there will be a large following of City supporters at Borough Park, despite the long trip involved.

The club has been flooded with enquires about travel details to the game and it is possible a coach may be arranged.

Friday 24th April 1964

CITY SUPPORTERS TRAVEL BY TRAIN AND COACH
Exeter City supporters face journeys of nearly 400 miles by road and rail tonight as they go on their way to the most important league match ever played by the club.

A train will leave Exeter St David's Station at 5.30pm with two through coaches added for the trip to Workington as supporters have taken advantage of the special return excursion fare of 70/-.

There will also be a further 40 supporters, members of the Grecians' Association, who will be making the journey by coach.

They are leaving Exeter at 11.30pm and estimate they will arrive in Workington at around 2.30pm tomorrow.

Saturday 25th April 1964

GOOD LUCK MESSAGES AWAIT CITY
When the Exeter City team arrived at their hotel in Carlisle last night, there were messages waiting for them, wishing good luck for the match against Workington today.

They included telegrams and cards from Belmont Bowling Club in Exeter and one from former Exeter City full back Bob Pollard. There was also one from a long distance fan in the Canary Islands.

When the City party reached the Borough Park ground of Workington, they found their dressing room table loaded with good luck telegrams from organisations and individuals., including one from the players of the Exeter Rugby Club.

Hundreds of Exeter City fans have made the long journey to Workington which should help create an atmosphere more akin to a cup tie.

Football League Game 46
Saturday April 25th
Borough Park
8600

Workington	0 v 0	Exeter City
Ower	1	Barnett
Chapman	2	Smyth
Lumsden	3	MacDonald
Murphy	4	Mitchell
Brow	5	Harvey
Burkinshaw	6	Anderson
Lowes	7	Rees
Carr	8	Banks
Hooper	9	Curtis
Moran	10	Hancock
Martin	11	Thorne

EXETER CITY ARE PROMOTED!!
'First Time in the Club's History'

The best kept secret of Exeter City's promotion winning goalless draw with Workington was that Alan Banks should not have played.

He was far from fit with his arm injury, but at the same time was desperate to play himself and it proved to be a great morale booster.

The game was a grim, grudging battle, which was only any kind of spectacle if one knew exactly how much hung on the outcome.

Everyone worked hard as City stuck to their highly successful plan of defending and waiting to make the odd breakaway attack.

It was a difficult game to start with as both sides were equally edgy and easily prone to mistakes.

With Arnold Mitchell marshalling his side wonderfully, the Grecians gradually settled down.

They only had two scoring chances in the whole game, but that did not matter. It was more important to keep Workington out for that vital point.

Co-ordinated covering from everyone saw to that efficiently and when Workington did get through with a shot or a header, Alan Barnett was on top form.

The last 15 minutes were the most harrowing, for if Workington had scored then, there would have been little time for City to recover, but they held on, and made club history in doing so, as they won promotion.

WORKINGTON
ASSOCIATION FOOTBALL CLUB LIMITED
Chairman: E. D. SMITH, J.P.

Manager: K. FURPHY. Secretary: NORMAN CONQUEST

Borough Park Tel. 2871

FOOTBALL LEAGUE FOURTH DIVISION

VISITORS

EXETER CITY

SATURDAY, 25th APRIL, 1964

KICK-OFF 3 p.m.

8,600 gate Draw 0-0

REDS FIGHTING FUND

Saturday, the 25th April, will be the last Match of this Season but not the end of the Daily Draw. We are well aware that without your support we would never have reached Third Division status and the Directors, Staff and Players of the Club would like to thank you for your help and look forward to a closer association in the future.

OFFICIAL PROGRAMME — 3d.

FOURTH DIVISION - 1963-64

	P	W	D	L	F	A	Pts
Gillingham	46	23	14	9	59	30	60
Carlisle United	46	25	10	11	113	58	60
Workington	46	24	11	11	76	52	59
Exeter City	46	20	18	8	62	37	58
Bradford City	46	25	6	15	76	62	56
Torquay United	46	20	11	15	80	54	51
Tranmere Rovers	46	20	11	15	85	73	51
Brighton & H.A.	46	19	12	15	71	52	50
Aldershot	46	19	10	17	83	78	48
Halifax Town	46	17	14	15	77	77	48
Lincoln City	46	19	9	18	67	75	47
Chester	46	19	8	19	65	60	46
Bradford P.A.	46	18	9	18	75	81	45
Doncaster Rovers	46	15	12	19	70	75	42
Newport County	46	17	8	21	64	73	42
Chesterfield	46	15	12	19	57	71	42
Stockport County	46	15	12	19	50	58	42
Oxford United	46	14	13	19	59	63	41
Darlington	46	14	12	20	66	93	40
Rochdale	46	12	15	19	56	59	39
Southport	*46*	*15*	*9*	*22*	*63*	*88*	*39*
York City	*46*	*14*	*7*	*25*	*52*	*66*	*35*
Hartlepools United	*46*	*12*	*9*	*25*	*54*	*93*	*33*
Barrow	*46*	*6*	*18*	*22*	*51*	*93*	*30*

WESTERN LEAGUE FINAL TABLE

	P	W	D	L	F	A	Pts
Bideford	42	30	6	6	113	36	68
Bristol City	42	24	15	3	122	434	63
Bridgwater Town	42	25	10	7	82	32	60
Welton Rovers	42	24	6	12	84	54	54
Dorchester Town	42	19	14	9	94	56	52
Salisbury City	42	21	8	13	80	61	50
Barnstaple Town	42	20	9	13	92	69	49
Minehead	42	20	8	14	96	85	48
Weymouth	42	16	12	14	94	74	44
Andover	42	17	10	15	89	78	44
Torquay United	42	18	7	17	81	73	43
Yeovil Town	42	17	9	16	73	99	43
Chippenham Town	42	15	8	19	75	82	38
Bath City	42	12	12	18	77	92	36
Frome Town	42	11	11	20	69	97	33
Weston-Super-Mare	42	11	11	20	58	86	33
Glastonbury	42	11	9	22	70	91	31
EXETER CITY	42	8	15	19	73	100	31
Poole Town	42	11	6	25	56	98	28
Bridport	42	7	14	21	40	100	28
Portland United	42	10	5	27	63	127	25
Taunton Town	42	8	9	25	37	105	25

EXETER CITY FOOTBALL & ATHLETIC
CO. LTD.

Regd. Office: St. James' Park, Exeter   Tel. 54073

President: S. H. THOMAS   Vice-President: J. RIGBY

Board of Directors:
Chairman: R. J. ROSE   Vice-Chairman: G. H. GILLIN
F. E. J. DART   L. W. KERSLAKE   J. RODGERS

Secretary — K. F. HONEY   Team Manager — J. EDWARDS

Honorary Medical Officer: Dr. G. L. STUMBLES

WESTERN LEAGUE
Exeter City 1 Chippenham Town 1
Scorer: Exeter City: Symington.

CELEBRATION TIME
"Up the City!" Tens of thousands of voices have been heard shout out this cry in over 50 years of football, but it is only now that it has found its true meaning for Exeter City, who are promoted to the Third Division.

They got there after 90 minutes of nail biting that was almost too much to bear for around 500 City supporters who had made the long journey to Workington on Saturday to witness the greatest day in Exeter City's Football League history.

The tension was so bad for some in the final 15 minutes of the match that they left their seats in the grandstand to go nearer to the touchline to shout City on.

When the final whistle sounded, pandemonium broke out, for Workington had got promotion as well.

Supporters swarmed onto the field in front of the stand, shouting and chanting their heroes names until each of the 22 players appeared in the directors' box.

Back in the Exeter City dressing room there were tots of whisky for the triumphant players, before they headed back to their hotel in Carlisle.

The champagne flowed as the City party celebrated. The hotel management had made a special cake in City's colours with 'Well done Exeter' iced on the top.

Many of the Exeter City supporters travelled back from Carlisle on the same train on Saturday night as the team.

They cheered the team onto the train and again at 12.30am on Crewe station as they and the players changed trains for Exeter.

Sunday 26th April 1964

It was the same when everyone got off at Exeter St David's on Sunday morning as they were joined by hundreds more.

Wearing scarves and rosettes, waving rattles and banners, cheering and shouting, the waiting crowd surged forward as the train pulled in.

They surrounded the players inside and outside the station for about half an hour, cheering for one and then another, carrying banners that read 'Thanks Banks and all the ranks.' and 'Grand show Exeter - now for Division Two.'

LES KERSLAKE: A LUCKY CHARM
Superstition plays a big part in football success or so the Exeter City players believe.

While they have been winning they have stuck strictly to routines that they have followed in previous weeks, even to sitting in exactly the same coach seat. or wearing a particular tie, even dressing in a particular order.

This has been extended to the boardroom where director, Les Kerslake, has been one of the team's 'Lucky Charms.'

He had missed only one away game since the end of October and they lost that one. So though he has been unable to get away early, he drove overnight to be at Workington and avoid breaking the sequence.

Monday 27th April 1964

CIVIC RECEPTION FOR EXETER CITY F.C.
Exeter City will continue their promotion celebrations this week with a Civic reception tonight at the Exeter Guildhall at 5.45pm.

They will also do a lap of honour before tomorrow's Devon Professional Bowl Final against Plymouth Argyle at St James' Park, before heading off for a private meal afterwards.

A reception meal and a stage introduction at the Odeon Cinema, Exeter, plus an invitation dinner will be fixed later in the week.

Club chairman Reg Rose said that although Exeter City had reached the Third Division, they did not want to stop there and that they were hoping this would be the beginning not the end.

There would be a policy meeting and also a finance meeting so that the club will know just how far it can expand.

Rose added that there would be a lot of changes by next season. They knew the weak spots and they would be remedied.

MAYOR CONGRATULATES CITY
A week of celebrations for Exeter City's promotion winning players started at the Guildhall last night with a civic reception given by the Mayor Of Exeter.

First team players, manager Jack Edwards and the whole board of directors were told by Mayor Alderman W.G. Daw:-

"As a former player myself and a keen supporter, I am delighted you have got promotion in my year of office.

"I congratulate all the players and I am sure that the city of Exeter is very proud of you indeed."

Tuesday 28th April 1964

NOW THE GRECIANS WIN THE DEVON BOWL
Devon Professional Bowl Final
Exeter City 4 Plymouth Argyle 0
Scorers: Exeter City: Thorne 3, Banks.
Attendance: 8,141
Exeter City team: Barnett, Smyth, MacDonald, Mitchell, Harvey, Hancock, Rees, Welsh, Banks, Curtis, Thorne.
Plymouth Argyle team: MacLaren, Baird, Fulton, Newman, Wyatt, Cobb, Corbett, Williams, Lord, Jackson, Jennings.

The highest attendance for a Devon Professional Bowl game turned up at St James' Park, and they were not disappointed as they saw Exeter City round off their best ever season by beating Plymouth Argyle, and therefore retaining the Bowl for the third season running.

Before the game commenced the Exeter City squad were cheered all the way around the ground as they did lap of honour in recognition of their promotion to the Third Division.

It was not until the 40th minute that supporters really got what they wanted, a goal from their hero, Alan Banks.

This was followed by two quick goals from ex-Argyle winger, Adrian Thorne, at the start of the second half.

Then Thorne became the first player this season to score a hat-trick in a first team game with another goal in the very last minute.

It was a complete triumph for the Grecians. They got the goals and were still defensively sound as ever.

They needed to be as Plymouth had their full Second Division line up out and when they got going they looked dangerous.

It was pleasing to see Eric Welsh back in the City side, during a season in which a cartilage operation restricted his playing opportunities.

It proved to be Exeter City's night again at the end of what has been a memorable season.

DOUBLE CELEBRATION DINNER
Two ardent Exeter City supporters, Dave Hancock and Ted Roberts entertained the players who took Exeter City into the Third Division to a celebration dinner at the

Buckerell Lodge Hotel, following the game against Plymouth Argyle.

It proved to be a double celebration as the players took along the Devon Professional Bowl which they won by defeating Plymouth Argyle 4-0.

Saturday 1st May 1964

SIXTEEN PLAYERS ARE RETAINED BY CITY
Sixteen of Exeter City's 23 professional playing staff have been retained and will go into the Third Division with the club next season.

Only one regular first team man finds himself on the transfer list and John Henderson is available for a fee of £3,000.

With him is John Edgar who is priced at £500, whilst George Spiers and Ray Gough are both listed at £250 each.

Free transfers have been given to goalkeeper Jimmy Parkhill, full-back Peter Quarrington and winger Brian Symington.

The retained list reads:-
Goalkeeper: Alan Barnett
Full-Backs: Cecil Smyth, Les MacDonald, Roy Patrick.
Half-Backs: Arnold Mitchell, Keith Harvey, Des Anderson, Dave Hancock, Derek Grace, Peter Rutley.
Forwards: Graham Rees, Alan Banks, Eric Welsh, Dermot Curtis, Adrian Thorne, George Ley.

ADMISSION CHARGES FOR NEXT SEASON
With Exeter City having reached the Third Division for 1964-65, the club announced that admission charges would be as follows:-

Ground: Adults 3s 6d; Boys 1s 9d.
Enclosure seats: Adults 5s.
Grandstand seats: 8s
Season tickets for the Grandstand: £8 - £1 discount if purchased before 31st May 1964.
Reserve team admission prices: Grandstand: 4s; Ground: Adults 2s; Boys 1s.

Alan Banks' Goals Fire City To Promotion

These days it seems it is way too easy to named as a legend at a football club. When you compare some of those who are bestowed that honour by supporters, they have achieved only a fraction of other players from the past.

Alan Banks is a true Exeter City legend, netting 101 goals in 258 league appearances, and he was, of course, a key member of the 1963-64 promotion winning team.

He fondly recalls the day that he signed for the Grecians, having scored a stack of goals for Southern League Cambridge City. although Liverpool still held his Football League registration.

"We travelled from Cambridge to Exeter by train and was met at Central station by club chairman, Les Kerslake.

*It seemed a long way from Cambridge, and in fact I didn't really know where Exeter was!"

"I wasn't happy with the terms first offered to me, and then Les asked if we would like to go for a drive around the area.

"He took us to Exmouth, where in contrast to the rain in Cambridge earlier that morning, the sun was shining and there was blue sky. There were people sat on the beach and outside their beach huts which we thought was absolutely great.

"We discussed terms again and this time everything was agreed and I signed. I even took the cheque for the transfer fee from Exeter City back to Cambridge City!"

Banks quickly settled into the Exeter team and showed what a good player he was scoring some vital goals, but when did he and the team really feel that promotion was a possibility?

"It was after we won 2-1 at Brighton and Hove Albion on Boxing Day. Adrian Thorne scored and I got the other.

"We felt if we could keep playing like we did, then promotion was a possibility, and we then went on a good run of results.

"We may not have been the greatest of teams, but we were well organised and that was down to manager Jack Edwards.

"He had us playing exactly the same at home and away and it worked. It got us the results we wanted."

The one downside of playing for Exeter City at that time were the long journeys for games in the north of England, and it has to be remembered that this was pre-motorway days.

"To give an example, " explained Banks, "For a game at Stockport County, we would leave Exeter at 8am. Then make a stop for coffee at Bristol Airport and on to Gloucester for lunch. Not arriving at Stockport until around 6pm."

A journey therefore of approximately ten hours, which today could be undertaken in less than five via the M5 and M6.

The Grecians needed a point to be certain of promotion as they travelled to Workington for the final match of the season, with the hosts being promoted as well.

Banks had missed the previous game due to a shoulder injury but wanted to take his place in the side at Workington and was given the go ahead to do so as the City team stayed overnight in Keswick prior to the match.

"To be honest it wasn't much of match," revealed Banks. "Both teams would be promoted if it was a draw and that is how it ended - goalless.

"Both sets of supporters invaded the pitch at the final whistle to celebrate and it took us some time before we were able to get back to the dressing room.

"The Workington directors brought in a case of champagne so that we could celebrate as well.

"We then headed off to Carlisle to a hotel where we had an evening meal. The Chef has made a large cake with 'congratulations iced on it.

"After travelling back to Exeter on the overnight train, we were greeted by hundreds of City fans at St David's station, both on the station itself and outside."

So Exeter City had ended the season by becoming the first team in the club's history to achieve promotion, and what a memorable season it had been!

On the next two pages are a copy of Alan's contract with Exeter City for season 1963/4.

P

An Agreement

made the TWENTYFIFTH day of OCTOBER 19 63 between Keith P. Honey

of St. James' Park, EXETER

in the COUNTY OF Devon

the Secretary of and acting pursuant to Resolution and Authority for and on behalf of the EXETER CITY FOOTBALL CLUB of St. James' Park, EXETER (hereinafter referred to as the Club) of the one part and ALLAN ALLOWS

of 13, Rectory Farm Estate, Cherry Hinton, CAMBRIDGE.

in the COUNTY OF Cambridge. Professional Football Player

(hereinafter referred to as the Player) of the other part Whereby it is agreed as follows:—

1. The Player hereby agrees to play in an efficient manner and to the best of his ability for the Club.

2. The Player shall attend the Club's ground or any other place decided upon by the Club for the purposes of or in connection with his training as a Player pursuant to the instructions of the Secretary, Manager, or Trainer of the Club, or of such other person, or persons as the Club may appoint. (This provision shall not apply if the Player is engaged by the Club at a weekly wage of less than One Pound or at a wage per match.)

3. The Player shall do everything necessary to get and keep himself in the best possible condition so as to render the most efficient service to the Club, and will carry out all the training and other instructions of the Club through its representative officials.

4. The Player shall observe and be subject to all the Rules, Regulations and Bye-Laws of The Football Association, and any other Association, League, or Combination of which the Club shall be a member. And this Agreement shall be subject to any action which shall be taken by The Football Association under their Rules for the suspension or termination of the Football Season, and if any such suspension or termination shall be decided upon the payment of wages shall likewise be suspended or terminated, as the case may be and in any proceedings by the Player against the Club it shall be a sufficient and complete defence by and answer by and on the part of the Club that such suspension or termination hereof is due to the action of The Football Association, or any Sub-Committee thereof to whom the power may be delegated.

5. The Player shall not engage in any business or live in any place which the Directors (or Committee) of the Club may deem unsuitable.

6. Unless this Agreement has previously been determined as hereinafter provided the Player shall not before the 9.5.65. approach or entertain approaches from any other Club or person with a view to changing his Club, unless otherwise agreed by the Club and Player. Under no cir-

tion shall be cancelled by this Association where necessary. Agreements between Clubs and Players shall contain a clause showing the provision made for dealing with such disputes and for the cancelling of the Agreements and Registrations by this Association. Clubs not belonging to any League or Combination before referred to may, upon obtaining the approval of this Association, make similar regulations. Such regulations to provide for a right of appeal by either party to the County Association, or to this Association.

13. In the event of the Club failing to fulfil the terms and conditions of this Agreement the Player may, on giving fourteen days notice to the Club, terminate this Agreement such notice to be in writing. The Player must forward a copy of the notice to The Football Association and the Club shall have the right of appeal within seven days to The Football Association, which may either dismiss such appeal, or allow the same, and, if so, on such terms and conditions as it may think fit.

14. The following special provisions laid down by the Competitions in which the Player will compete are accepted by and will be observed by the Player:—

(1) It is hereby agreed by the player that if he shall at any time be absent from his duties by reason of sickness or injury he shall, during such absence, be entitled to receive only the difference between the weekly wage he was receiving at the time of his sickness or injury, and the amount he receives as benefit under the National Insurance Act, 1946, or The National Insurance (Industrial Injuries) Act, 1946, and for the purpose of this Clause his wages shall be deemed to accrue from day to day.

(2) If at any time during the period of this agreement the payments herein agreed shall be in excess of the payments permitted to be paid by the Club to the player in accordance with the Regulations of The Football League the payments to the player shall be the amount the Club is entitled to pay by League Regulations in force from time to time, and this Agreement shall be read and construed as if it were varied accordingly.

(3) The player agrees that he will not without the written permission of the Club grant interviews to nor write articles for newspapers or other publications nor take part in television or radio programmes and that he will submit such articles etc. to the Club for approval before allowing publication of the same.

15. Basic Wages.

£30.0.0. per week from 25.10.63. to 2.5.64.
£25.0.0. per week from 3.5.64. to 1.8.64.
£30.0.0. per week from 2.8.64. to 9.5.65.
£25.0.0. per week from 10.8.65. to 30.6.65.
£ per week from to
£ per week from to
£ per week from to
£ per week from to

16. Other financial provisions:—
(Fill in as required.) Plus a Crowd Incentive Bonus, based on paying spectators at Home matches, of 10s.0d. at 5,000., with a further 10s.0d. for each complete 500. thereafter, and usual bonuses.

Jack Edwards

Des Anderson

Alan Banks

Alan Barnett

Exeter City Players and Management 1963/64

The Manager - John William 'Jack' Edwards

There is no denying that the name of Jack Edwards will forever be in the record books of Exeter City Football Club, as he became the first ever manager to lead the Grecians to promotion to the Third Division in 1964.

Described by his players as a well organised individual, this was reflected in the team that he put out on the pitch, the players knowing exactly what was expected of them.

It was therefore a huge blow to the club when Edwards resigned in January 1965 after he had taken, quite rightly, umbrage at the fact that a chief scout, Ellis Stuttard, had been appointed by the board of directors without his knowledge.

Born in Risca, Monmouthshire, 6th July 1929, his first club as a player was Cardiff City, where he signed amateur forms. The full-back then moved to Lovells Athletic before gaining his first full professional contract with Crystal Palace in September 1949.

After 223 league outings, Edwards was transferred to Rochdale in June 1959, where in two seasons he added a further 68 appearances.

He was appointed player coach at Ashford Town in the summer of 1961, finally arriving at Exeter City as their trainer twelve months later.

Edwards became caretaker manager at Exeter in February 1963, and soon showed his ability as a manager as under his guidance the team climbed from 22nd in the Fourth Division to 17th, in a season that did not end until well into May, it having been extended following one of the worst winters in living memory that led to a catalogue of postponements.

Not surprisingly Edwards was offered and became manager in May 1963. What a master stroke that proved to be as the team enjoyed success in the Fourth Division,

After leaving Exeter City, Edwards was trainer at Torquay United between 1965 and 1971. This included a spell as caretaker manager in December 1968.

Edwards was appointed manager at Torquay United in October 1971, remaining in charge until January 1973.

He was to return for a second brief spell as trainer at Exeter City in 1973, then followed City manager Bobby Saxton to take a similar position at Plymouth Argyle. He later became a scout for Leeds United.

Anderson, John Desmond (b:Downpatrick, 11th September 1940)

Anderson had been signed by the Grecians from Northern Irish side, Glenavon, in August 1962.

He had previously made his name at amateur level going on to win seven caps for the Northern Ireland amateur international team.

Appearing for Cliftonville and then Glenavon in the Irish League, Anderson played in a trial match at Exeter City before agreeing to sign a full contract with the Grecians in August 1962.

Highly thought of, he went straight into Exeter City's first team following regular centre-half Keith Harvey's ankle fracture, making his league debut in the opening game of the season at home to Torquay United, a match that the Plainmoor club won 3-0.

Such was his consistency that Anderson played in all but two matches that season and then never missed a match during the 1963-64 promotion season, forming part of the formidable half-back line of Arnold Mitchell, Keith Harvey and Des Anderson, that virtually picked itself every game.

Players often worked during the summer months to supplement their basic wages, and in the 1964 close season Anderson became an interior decorator to supplement his summer wages.

Anderson was to again show his consistency by missing only three league games in the 1964-65 season, although the team found it more of a struggle in the Third Division.

He also scored what was to be his only goal netted for the Grecians during a 4-1 victory against Grimsby Town at St. James' Park.

The substitute rule was first introduced in season 1965-66, when a team could use a player to replace another only if an injury had occurred.

The honour of being the Grecians very first playing substitute went to Anderson, who was introduced against Brighton and Hove Albion at the Goldstone Ground. He replaced the injured Bryce Fulton, as the City lost the match 2-1.

It was a season in which Exeter suffered relegation back to the Fourth Division and Anderson was to only feature in a handful of matches.

Having asked for a transfer in September 1965, Anderson was released at the end of the season and signed for Chesterfield on a free transfer in July 1966.

At the time of asking for a transfer, Anderson had considered moving to South Africa to live, having studied for a qualification in Industrial Management.

Anderson's two-season stay with Chesterfield resulted in him featuring in just 8 league matches for the club and in the summer of 1968 he remained in the area, signing for Matlock Town.

Living in North Wales in 2011, Anderson paid a return visit to St James' Park in March of that year, the first time he had been back since he played for the Grecians.

Banks, Alan (b:Liverpool, 5th October 1938)

It is probably fair to say that had Exeter City not parted with what was then, one of their highest transfer fees to sign Alan Banks when they did, then the club would not have won promotion in 1964.

His exceptional goalscoring ability and energetic style of play made him a firm favourite with the City fans, and in two spells with the club he became one of the Exeter City legends.

After playing for the Rankin Boys Club in his home town of Liverpool, Banks was signed as amateur by the Anfield club, becoming a full professional with them in May 1958.

He appeared in a handful of first team league matches, when he scored an impressive six goals in eight appearances.

Banks couldn't win a regular place in the side though and he was allowed to join Southern League Cambridge City, with Liverpool retaining his Football League registration.

His goalscoring record at Cambridge was nothing short of sensational as he scored 129 goals in two and a half seasons.

With Exeter manager Jack Edwards seeking a proven goalscorer in his team's push for promotion, he signed Banks for fees totalling £5,250.

The Grecians had to pay Cambridge City an initial £3,000, plus a further £250 after 20 first team appearances. They also had to part with £2,000 to Liverpool who still held his Football League registration.

Banks was an immediate success at St. James' Park, and not only did his goals fire the team to promotion but he also not surprisingly ended the season as top scorer with 18 league goals. One wonders how many he would have got had he started the season with the Grecians?

The following season in the Third Division, Banks once again got amongst the goals, but disaster struck both for him personally and the club when playing in a match against Port Vale in February 1965. Banks sustained a broken leg and he proved to be huge loss to the team.

Banks was leading goalscorer for Exeter City on four occasions, his first stay at St James' Park ending as he joined arch rivals Plymouth Argyle in May 1966, making the move with goalkeeper Peter Shearing for a joint fee of £7,750.

He never reproduced the same rich vein of form at Home Park though and after 5 goals in 19 league matches, he was on his way back to Exeter City in November 1967. when he was re-signed along with John Newman (later to become manager of the Grecians) for a joint fee of £8,000.

Banks soon hit the back of the net once more, as if he had never been away, and was the Exeter City Player of the Year in 1968-69.

It just got better as Banks scored 21 goals in 1970-71. It was in that season that he broke the club's individual scoring record for City when he netted his 90th Grecians' goal in a game against York City in February 1971 at Bootham Crescent, beating the previous 89-goal record held by Graham Rees.

All things must come to an end and Banks was given a free transfer by City at the end of the 1972-73 season and he joined Southern League Poole Town.

Banks made one more appearance at St James' Park though when he returned to play for Exeter City in his own testimonial match against Leicester City in May 1975.

A month later he signed for Tiverton Town, having been released by Poole, despite being their Player of the Year. He continued to live in Exeter and later worked for Exsports at the Guildhall Shopping Centre.

A terrific character, full of enthusiasm for the game, Banks also helped organise matches for the ex-Exeter City players team and continued to attend matches at St James' Park as a spectator.

Barnett, Alan George Samuel (b: Croydon 4th November 1934)

Barnett commenced his goalkeeping career with local side Croydon Amateurs, from whom he joined Portsmouth in September 1955, who gave him his first opportunity at Football League level.

He was to feature in 25 league matches for Pompey before moving to Grimsby Town in December 1958, where he won a fairly regular place in the first team, making 116 league appearances.

Exeter City manager Jack Edwards moved swiftly to get the signature of Barnett after the player had been given a free transfer and he moved to the Grecians in July 1963.

Barnett made his debut for Exeter against Bradford City at Valley Parade the following month, and it was a start of a run of matches that saw him only miss one throughout the whole promotion winning campaign.

Barnett, who had been subject of an enquiry in August 1965 from Swansea about possibly signing for them, lost his place to Peter Shearing in the Third Division in 1965-66 and by the end of the season had been released by the Grecians to join neighbours Torquay United in June 1966.

Despite his successful stay at Exeter, the same could not be said about his time at Plainmoor as he failed to make a single league outing for the Gulls and was released at the end of 1966-7

Barnett later worked for his father-in-law who owned a Garden Centre in Portsmouth. He died in October 1978, aged just 43.

Cochrane, John James (b:Belfast 11th May 1944)

A winger who had previously played for Brighton and Hove Albion, where he had gained his first professional contract in October 1961.

During his time on the south coast, Cochrane scored one goal in 14 league outings and then moved to Exeter City on a free transfer in August 1963.

Cochrane was to feature just twice for Exeter, his debut coming against Lincoln City in August 1963. He retained his place in the side for the next match against Gillingham.

His stay at St James' Park was a short one though and he had left long before the team was celebrating promotion to the Third Division in the 1963-64 season, having returned to Ireland to sign for Ards in September 1963.

Still playing for Ards in September 1967, it was reported that Cochrane had stated that he had eyesight problems when he played for Exeter and at times was unable to follow the ball!

The problem was solved when he joined Ards as he was given smaller and stronger contact lenses and he said he was a like a new man.

Curtis, Dermot Patrick (b: Dublin 26th August 1932)

If Alan Banks was the goalscorer of the team, then Dermot Curtis was without doubt the one player who added class to the side.

Curtis was playing in the League of Ireland for Shelbourne when he made his full international debut (and scored) for the Republic of Ireland at home to Denmark on 3rd October 1956. The first of 17 full caps.

Dermot Curtis

Derek Grace

In December that year he joined Bristol City where he was to score 16 league goals in only 26 games.

In September 1958, Curtis was transferred to Ipswich Town, playing in the side that won promotion to Division One in 1961, and the League Championship the following season.

In August 1963 he moved to Exeter City for a bargain £1,000, and a month later, became the first Exeter player to win a full cap for his country in a 0-0 draw with Austria in Vienna.

Curtis asked for a transfer in September 1965 and the following January a delegation from Dundalk FC arrived in Exeter to offer him a move there for a fee of £800. Curtis turned the move down.

After 91 league appearances (in which he scored 23 goals), Curtis moved to Torquay United, signing in August 1966.

However, his move to Plainmoor was not a great success as in his only season he made just 12 league appearances, scoring just a single goal.

In June 1967 he returned to Exeter City, where his league career was to end after a further 66 league appearances in which he scored 10 goals.

He later played Western League football for Bideford, signing for them in July 1969, and captaining the side that won the Championship in 1970-71. He later had a spell as player-manager of Elmore.

After retiring from playing Curtis was a panel beater, being employed in Locomotors in Sidwell Street, Exeter.

After a long illness, Curtis died in November 2008, aged 64.

Edgar, John (b: Worsborough Dale 9th April 1936)

Edgar was to feature in only half a dozen games during the promotion season, and never did reproduce his goalscoring ability that he had shown at his previous clubs.

He started his career with Barnsley in May 1954. After making 22 league appearances and scoring six goals, he joined Gillingham in June 1958.

After making 45 league appearances and scoring 23 goals for the Gills, he then moved to York City in June 1959.

He scored the club's quickest hat-trick, after scoring three goals in six minutes in a 3-0 win over Accrington Stanley and finished the 1959-60 season as the club's top scorer, after scoring 17 goals.

His appearances the following season were curtailed by a serious injury and he moved to Hartlepools United in June 1961 where he netted 31 goals in 72 league outings.

Signing for Exeter City on a free transfer in July 1963, he made his debut in a 2-1 win at Bradford City on the opening day of the season.

On leaving St James' Park after just one season, Edgar joined Matlock Town. He died in February 2008.

Grace, Derek George (b: Chiswick 29th December 1944)

Originally an apprentice with Queen's Park Rangers, it was Exeter City who gave a full professional contract to Grace when they signed him on a free transfer in May 1962.

He had to wait quite some time for his debut however, which was the only league match he played in the first season with the club, against Rochdale at Spotland in April 1963.

Grace was to play a major part in the promotion success of 1963-64 though, as he scored four goals in 32 starts.

He asked for a transfer in May 1964, but two months later came off the list. However by January 1965 he was back on it again.

The 1964-65 season in the Third Division didn't prove to be as successful for the player and he only made a handful of outings, before being released on a free transfer.

Grace then signed for Gillingham in July 1965, where he played four league games in his one season stay at Priestfield.

After leaving the Gills he moved to Margate in 1967, whilst working as a teacher at a school in Bromley.

Grace went on to make a total of 154 appearances for Margate, scoring 38 goals. he then joined Dartford at the start of the 1969-70 season, scoring nine goals in 59 appearances.

In July 1970, Grace signed for Berea Park, a side based in Pretoria, South Africa.

He also appeared in a few matches for Maidstone United during the 1972-73 season before setting off on his travels again joining Canadian team, London City.

Returning to England he linked up with Gravesend and Northfleet for 1973-74, and then later played for Herne Bay in 1976-77. He was living in Cape Town, South Africa in 2008.

Hancock, David Jeffrey (b. Exeter 24th July 1938

One of the select band of players who have appeared for all three of Devon's Football League clubs. Although born in Exeter, it was with Plymouth Argyle that he began his career as a junior, signing a full contract in September 1955.

He had attended Hele's School where he won rugby union international honours playing for the England Schools side at scrum half.

After just two league appearances for Argyle, Hancock made the short move to Torquay United in January 1959, where he added 177 league appearances, scoring twelve goals. He was also a member of the 1959-60 promotion winning side.

He moved to Exeter City on transfer deadline day in March 1964 for a fee of £1,000, having been on the transfer list at Plainmoor after losing his place in the Torquay side.

Hancock played his part in helping the Grecians win promotion for the first time in their history at the end of the 1963-64 season, having made his debut for City in a 3-2 home win over Oxford United.

He netted three goals in 31 league outings the following season in the Third Division. After that he turned an offer to play in Canada with Toronto-based club, Roma in May 1965, who had offered him £30 per week.

He then left the club to emigrate to South Africa where he played for Durban United, signing a two-year deal with them in March 1966. He went on to play for South African teams Corinthians and Southern Suburbs after Durban United.

Hancock died in July 2007.

Harvey, William Keith (b. Crediton 25th December 1934)

A truly magnificent servant to Exeter City who played in well over 500 league and cup matches for the club.

Only one other player has appeared in more games for the Grecians - Arnold Mitchell - and they were to partner each other in City sides for many seasons.

Signing professional for Exeter in August 1952, Harvey made his league debut in a goalless draw at Bristol Rovers a month later.

It wasn't until season 1954-55 that Harvey won a regular place in the side, taking over the centre-half spot from Fred Davey.

Dave Hancock

Keith Harvey

George Ley

Lincoln City offered Exeter a player in exchange for Harvey in September 1956, but this was turned down. Harvey had a joint benefit match with Arnold Mitchell in April 1957 when Exeter City played an Manager's All Star XI.

He sustained a broken leg in October 1958 and also a broken ankle in a pre-season match in August 1962, but he fought back on each occasion to become a member of the 1963-64 promotion winning side, a season in which he was an ever-present. He became Exeter City Player of the Year in 1965-66.

Appointed trainer at Exeter in July 1966, he still continued to play and gave up the position of trainer after just one year.

However, he again turned to training players after his own playing career came to an end.

Leaving Exeter in December 1972, he became a postman in his home town of Crediton. He then worked for the Post Office in Worthing from 1981.

In 2009. Harvey returned to St James' Park from his Petersfield home for a reunion of the 1964 promotion winning squad.

Henderson, John (b. Johnshaven 22nd September 1941)

A tall inside-forward with a powerful shot, Henderson was introduced to the Football League by Charlton Athletic who had signed the player from Scottish junior side, Montrose Victoria in June 1959. He went on to feature in four league games and scored one goal.

Henderson moved to Exeter City in November 1962 for a four-figure fee, the Grecians having tracked the player for some time after he had scored 30 goals for Charlton's reserves in 1961-62.

He didn't have the best of debuts for City lining up in a 4-0 defeat at Newport County, but went on to net eight goals in 28 starts.

He started off in the promotion team of 1963-4, but lost his place with the arrival of Alan Banks in October 1963, ending the season with six goals in 22 league appearances.

In November 1963, Henderson had asked the City directors permission to take up part-time employment as a carpenter, whilst continuing to play for the club, but this was refused.

He was placed on the transfer list by City in February 1964, and a month later Southern League Cheltenham Town offered £1,000 plus 50 % of any future fee they got for the player. The move was turned down by Henderson and he came off the transfer list.

After turning down further offers from Gillingham, Cambridge City and Barrow (the latter two clubs in June 1964), he eventually moved to Doncaster Rovers in July 1964 for £750, but Henderson only stayed with them for one season, failing to hit the target in ten league outings.

He then spent the 1965-66 season with Chesterfield, playing in 28 league games and scoring three goals.

Linking up with Kidderminster Harriers, Henderson became a regular scorer for them and something of a legend, netting 144 goals in 333 matches.

Henderson then played for Stourbridge, Halesowen Town and Dudley Town whom he joined in December 1977. In 2004 he was reported to have won a golf tournament in Habberley, Worcestershire.

Ley, Oliver Albert George

Although born locally in Exminster, Ley was signed by Exeter City in September 1963 after a successful trial period. He had previously played for Hitchin Town and had been on the books at Arsenal.

It was to prove to be an astute signing, as he made his league debut for the Grecians against Carlisle United at St James' Park in the same month. He was member of the promotion winning side in his first season.

Ley was a left-winger then, but the Grecians converted him to left-back, and it was in that position that he excelled and played the majority of his games with City, although he didn't start in a defensive position until the 1965-66 season.

Swansea enquired about the availability of Ley in June 1966 and seven months later the player asked for a transfer.

He was transferred to Portsmouth in May 1967 for a fee of £8,000 and went on to score ten goals in 184 league outings for the Fratton Park club.

He then joined Brighton and Hove Albion in September 1972 where he added a further 47 league appearances.

After spending some time playing for Dallas in Texas, Ley moved back to the Football League to sign for Gillingham in August 1974 and he stayed at the Priestfield Stadium for two years, during which time he scored three goals in 87 league appearances.

After leaving the Gills, Ley played for St Patrick's Athletic in the Republic of Ireland. He later returned to the USA and joined Dallas Tornado, before moving to Wichita Wings.

Les MacDonald

Arnold Mitchell

Ley became head youth coach at Luton Town in January 1990. He was then head coach of Austin Socadillos in the USA and served as Director of Coaching for the River City Rangers from 1996–2003. He then became Director of Coaching for the Crossfire Soccer Club. He was living in Austin, Texas in 2009.

MacDonald, Leslie (b. Newcastle 2nd April 1934)

Although hailing from the North East, MacDonald started his football career on the south coast as an apprentice with Portsmouth.

He signed a full contract for them in May 1955, but after two seasons and without having made a league outing, he joined Exeter City in June 1957, for a fee of £200 plus 50% of any future fee received by the Grecians.

This was the start of a lengthy stay at St James' Park, including playing in the Fourth Division promotion winning team of 1963-64.

He made his Grecians debut against Southend United on the opening day of the 1957-58 season, a game that ended in a 5-0 home defeat!

By the middle of the season though, MacDonald had become a regular fixture in the left-back spot and continued to be so for much of his stay with the Grecians.

After the team were relegated at the end of the 1965-66 season, MacDonald was one of several players to be given free transfers and he signed for Weymouth. After just one season with Weymouth, MacDonald moved on to sign for Gloucester City.

Living in Grays, Essex in 2009, MacDonald returned to St James' Park for a 1964 promotion winning team reunion.

Mitchell, Arnold (b. Rawmarsh 1st December 1929)

It is doubtful whether anyone will play as many Football League games for Exeter City as Mitchell. A player, and captain of the team, who really drove his side on at every opportunity.

Noted mainly for his defensive roles in the team, he played in every position, including taking over between the posts when the keeper was injured.

Originally on the books as an amateur with Sheffield Wednesday, he earned his first professional contract with Derby County in February 1948, but never made the first team breakthrough.

Moving on to Nottingham Forest in March 1950, and then Notts County in May 1951, he finally made his league debut when playing just once for the latter club.

It wasn't until he signed for Exeter City in July 1952 that he won a regular berth in the team, making his debut a month later in a home fixture against Northampton Town.

Playing in a variety of positions, he eventually settled into a wing-half role and was noted for his drive and encouragement of team mates, which inevitably led him to becoming captain.

In October 1962 he was appointed Exeter City's assistant lottery organiser and combined that role with that of playing.

Mitchell was a member of the Exeter team that won promotion for the first time in the club's history in 1964, when he netted three goals in 38 league starts.

His career by that time was coming to an end at St James' Park though, however, he did feature in 43 league games in 1964-65, and although linked with the manager's job at one time, he was released on a free transfer at the end of the 1965-66 season. He had actually asked for a transfer in March 1966.

He then signed for Taunton Town and unfortunately sustained a broken leg, the first major injury of his long career.

This effectively ended his playing days, but he continued to reside in Exeter and made the occasional return visit to St James' Park.

Mitchell, who joined the Dawlish Warren Golf Club in 1957, and represented them in various tournaments, was made a Life Member in 2011.

Northcott, George Edward (b. Torquay 7th May 1935)

Working at the Longpark Pottery on Newton Road, Torquay, Northcott joined Torquay United as a junior, where his elder brother Tommy was already an established first team player.

He turned professional in October 1952, but had to wait until the 1954-55 season for his league debut. He played 160 times for Torquay and was a member of their promotion winning team in 1959-60, before leaving at the end of the 1961-62 season

He joined Southern League, Cheltenham Town in the summer of 1962, and also played in their promotion winning team, but in August 1963 moved back into the Football League with Exeter City for a fee of £500.

However, he was to make just the one league appearance for the Grecians, lining up against York City at St James' Park in a 1-0 win in October 1963.

After leaving City he rejoined Cheltenham Town for a second spell at the club. On retiring from playing he worked in the construction and cleaning industry. He later became caretaker at Audley Park School in Torquay.

Northcott, in later years, suffered from Alzheimer's Disease and died in November 2010.

Parkhill, James Archibald (b. Belfast 27th July 1934

Parkhill began his career with Banbridge Town. He moved to senior football with Bangor in 1958. before moving to Cliftonville the following season.

A Northern Ireland Junior international goalkeeper, he was capped twice as an Amateur international in 1963.

He then moved to Exeter City, but played just once for the Grecians as they won promotion from the Fourth Division in 1964, making his debut in a 3-1 home win over Newport County in April 1964.

Released at the end of that season by the Grecians, Parkhill signed for Taunton Town and later returned to Northern Ireland.

Patrick, Roy (b. Overseal 4th December 1935)

A classy, underrated, defender who began his career in the junior sides at Derby County. He signed professional forms in February 1952 and went on to make 49 league appearances for the club.

He joined rivals, Nottingham Forest in May 1959 and added a further 57 league outings to his tally. Moving to the south coast and Southampton in June 1961, Patrick only managed 31 league appearances in the two seasons at The Dell.

He moved to Exeter City in March 1963 and made his debut against in a 3-1 home win over Hartlepool United, going on to feature in every game until the end of the season.

He was a member of the Grecians promotion winning squad of 1964, but only featured in 7 league games.

Patrick asked for a transfer in October 1963 and then sustained a back injury in March 1964 which ended his season.

He fared much better in 1964-65 playing in 25 league games, but with his contract at an end, was then released and he joined Burton Albion. Patrick died in 1998.

Phoenix, Peter Patrick (b. Urmston 31st December 1936)

Roy Patrick

Peter Rutley

Although Phoenix played his part in the first ever Exeter City team to win promotion in 1963-64, his stay at St James' Park was a short one, as it was reported he could not settle in Devon and missed his friends in the North of England.

He was playing for Tamworth when Oldham Athletic gave him his first Football League contract in February 1958.

He was a regular in the Oldham team and went on to make 161 league appearances, scoring 26 goals.

Transferred to Rochdale in October 1962, Phoenix stayed for 12 months, during which time he netted four goals in 36 league outings.

Signing for Exeter City in October 1963 for £1,400, he made his debut in a goalless draw at St James' Park against Halifax Town.

He was to appear in 15 consecutive league matches, with his only goal for the club being netted against Tranmere Rovers in a 5-0 home win.

Hankering for a return North, Phoenix jumped at the chance of moving to Southport in January 1964 for a fee of £625, where he only stayed for six months, playing in 10 league matches.

His next move was to Stockport County in July 1964, but again his stay was fairly brief, as he added a further 19 league outings and one goal, and at the end of that season he was released, to join Witton Albion. Phoenix then had a short spell with Wigan Athletic before moving to Bangor City for the 1966-67 season.

Rees, John Graham (b. Pontypridd 28th August 1937)

Rees became one of a number of players during the 1950s to have been spotted playing in junior football in South Wales and attending trials at Exeter City in August 1954.

After featuring in the City reserve team, Rees signed part-time professional forms in September 1954 for what was to be the start of a long association with the club.

He made his league debut in the same month for the Grecians in a 3-0 defeat at Norwich City. Rees was selected to appear in a trial match played at Newport for the Wales Under-23 side in February 1958.

By season 1958-59, Rees was a regular first teamer, missing just two matches, and scoring 23 goals, forming a lethal partnership with Ted Calland who netted 27 as City just missed out on promotion from the Fourth Division.

Rees was leading goalscorer for the Grecians in 1959-60 and 1960-61, and was a member of Exeter City's first ever promotion winning squad of 1963-64.

Cecil Smyth

Adrian Thorne

After nearly 12 years with the club, Rees was released at the end of the 1965-66 season and signed for Yeovil Town at the same time as his Grecians' team mate Alan Riding.

He turned down an offer to sign for Bideford in October 1967, and moved to Bridgwater Town instead.

After retiring from playing he worked as an accountant at Cardiff University.

Rutley, Peter (b. Exeter 19th May 1946)

Rutley was highly thought of as he progressed via the apprentice ranks (signed July 1961) to sign his first full contract at Exeter City in July 1963.

He made his league debut whilst still an apprentice when lining up in a 1-0 home win over Workington on 20th September 1962, aged 16 and four months, the youngest debutant since Cliff Bastin.

The following season he appeared at Halifax Town in October 1963, playing once more that season in the following game at home to York City as he helped the side win promotion for the first time in the club's history.

He was to feature in a further six Third Division matches in 1964-65 season, before being given a free transfer.

Rutley signed for Leicester City in August 1965 and was loaned to Wimbledon two months later, making 2 appearances.

He then joined Poole Town for the 1968-69 season, before moving to Margate in summer of 1969 going on to make 67 appearances, scoring five goals. He left club in August 1970 and moved to Somerset to live. By 1978 he was living in Poole and was still there in 2012.

Smyth, Cecil (b. Belfast 4th May 1941)

Smyth was a member of the Exeter City 1964 promotion team, and was one of several players who was signed from Irish clubs in the early 60s, having moved from Distillery to link up with the Grecians in August 1962.

The Belfast-born player quickly made a first team breakthrough making his Football League debut against Brentford at Griffin Park in September 1962.

After that he was pretty well a permanent member of the City first team and in 1963-64 missed just two matches as Exeter clinched promotion to the Third Division,

Smyth only scored once for Exeter, so it was fitting that it proved to be the winner in a 1-0 home win over York City in October 1963.

He asked for a transfer in December 1964. in Mar 1966 and again in January 1967. However, he stayed at Exeter until making the short move to Torquay United in August 1969 for what seemed a bargain fee of £2,500.

He never recaptured the sort of form he had so consistently displayed with Exeter and only made 23 league outings for the Plainmoor club before being released.

He was to later return to St James' Park where he played a number of reserve team matches using his vast experience to help nurture the younger players in the side.

Smyth was a quick tackling full-back, who had knack of recovering in an instant, and rolling over into a ball before standing upright again.

After retiring from playing he worked for the Prison Service in Exeter. He died on 7th November 2008.

Spiers, George Smyth (b. Belfast 3rd September 1941)

Spiers became one of a number of players to be recruited from Ireland by Exeter City in the early 1960s. He joined from Crusaders in August 1963 for a fee of £500 plus 25% of any future fee that the Grecians got for the player.

He made his league debut for City against in a 2-1 win at Bradford City the same month as he signed.

Although he featured n the opening three games of what was a promotion season for the Grecians, he only got another two outings.

Spiers was transfer listed in February 1964 and at the end of the season joined Port Elizabeth in South Africa. He continued to play in South Africa, joining Westview Apollon in 1967, but a year later moved to Bloemfontein City.

Thorne, Adrian Ernest (b. Brighton 2nd August 1937)

Thorne began his career with his local club, Brighton Grammarians in the Sussex County League.

Signed by Brighton and Hove Albion, and playing for their junior sides, he eventually signed a full contract in August 1954. He went on to score 38 goals in 76 league matches.

In only his fifth match for the first team, Thorne netted five goals in a 6-1 home win over Watford, to equal a club scoring record that had stood for 37 years.

He then moved to Plymouth Argyle in June 1961 for a fee of £8,000, but only played 11 league matches for them, netting two goals.

Thorne signed for Exeter City in December 1963 for a fee of £1,500 and made his debut for the Grecians in a 4-1 home win over Bradford City. Helping Exeter to promotion he was an ever present for the rest of the season.

He didn't get another first team chance though until the second half of the following season and in July 1965 he moved to Leyton Orient on a free transfer.

Whilst at Orient, Thorne studied at a teacher training college where he obtained an honours degree specialising in exercise physiology, and also he was to gain an FA senior coaching badge.

Thorne had just one season with Orient making two league outings, then moving on to Cheltenham Town, before returning to London to link up with Barnet.

Off the field and after retiring from playing, Thorne taught science as well as P.E. and in 2001 was Head of Department at St George's, Maida Vale, London.

Unfortunately he was suffering from osteo-arthritis which required two operations on his right ankle and in 2001 was living in Twickenham.

EXETER CITY RESERVE PLAYERS

The following players appeared for the Exeter City reserve team, other than those listed in the player profiles. Unfortunately, we have not been able to trace a handful of Christian names:-

Peter Arbury - Full-back - Later to become an apprentice.
Malcolm Clark - Forward - Trialist from Frimley Green, Surrey.
??? Dodd - Winger - Local amateur.
Colin Edmunds - Half-back - Local amateur who later played for Barnstaple Town.
Walter Gerrard - Forward - Trialist. Scotsman who had been with Barnsley as a youngster but returned to Scotland to play for Possil YM. Later played Scottish League football for ES Clydebank, East Stirlingshire and Berwick Rangers.
??? Gillard - Half-back - Local amateur.
Ray Gough - Half-back - Later played in Canada.
??? Howells - Half-back - Trialist.
??? May - Goalkeeper - Local amateur.
Terry Parker - Full-back - Trialist form the Weymouth area.
Keith Parsons - Half-back - Local amateur, who went on to play for Taunton Town.
Ian Pope - Half-back - Local amateur.
Peter Quarrington - Full-back - Later to become an apprentice.
Barry Redwood - Forward - Made one first team appearance in the Football League Cup.
Alan Riding - Forward - Went on to play for Yeovil Town.
Barry Sidey - Goalkeeper - Local amateur.

Bruce Stuckey - Winger - Later signed on a full contract and went on to play for Sunderland, Torquay United and AFC Bournemouth.
John Symington - Forward - Trialist from Belfast.
Bob Thompson - Goalkeeper - Trialist
Eric Welsh - Winger - Later to win international honours for Northern Ireland, as well as playing for Carlisle United, Torquay United and Hartlepool.
Adrian Williams - Forward - Trialist from Bristol City.

AN INTERVIEW WITH ... GRAHAM REES

A player who spent 12-years at Exeter City, after being signed as a 17-year-old in September 1954, Graham Rees went on to give the Grecians tremendous service, and became leading goalscorer in both 1959-60 and 1960-6i.

He played a major part in the 1963-64 promotion season, missing just one league game, at home to Chester in February 1964.

Now living in the Cardiff area, and a season ticket holder for Cardiff City, Graham has fond memories of his time at Exeter, especially the promotion winning team.

"Although I was really a left winger, and more comfortable there, I played on the right throughout the 1963-64 season. I even kept Eric Welsh out of the side, and he was to go on to play for Northern Ireland when he later moved to Carlisle United," said Graham.

'I also had to play defensively as well when needed, for right-back Cecil Smyth used to bomb forward when the opportunity arose and I had to drop back as cover."

Manager Jack Edwards, who had been appointed after the big freeze of Winter 1963, was no stranger to Graham.

"Jack had been a right-back at Crystal Palace and I had played against him a few times for Exeter. He joined City as trainer, but took over as manager from Cyril Spiers when he left the club.

"He was his own man. He had been a steady player during his career, but as a manager he got the team well organised.

"I remember once when he dropped Dermot Curtis from the team, which was a real shock, and we lost the next game.

"He called all the players in on the Sunday morning, which was very unusual, and instead of giving those who played a roasting, he turned to Dermot and had a go at him, even though he didn't play!

"Dermot was a quality player. But our season really changed when Alan Banks was signed and he was the one player we relied upon to score goals, which he did.

"Adrian Thorne, who came to the club later in the season, was also a very good player and helped us to promotion.

"The defence virtually picked itself. Barnett, Smyth, MacDonald, Mitchell, Harvey, Anderson. The forward line was switched around a bit from game to game.

"Arnold Mitchell really drove the team on. He was a motivator on the pitch. Whilst Keith Harvey was a 'rock' in the defence."

Recalling the final month of the season, which was to end in great success, it didn't seem like that was going to happen at one stage.

"We lost at home to Bradford Park Avenue, which seemed a disaster at the time, but then the very next game also at St James' Park, we thrashed Chesterfield 6-1 and I got one of the goals.

"This meant that we had to get at least a point at Workington in our last game to be absolutely sure of being promoted, although the one team that could have overtaken us had to win something like 26-0!"

Exeter duly drew 0-0 at Workington, and both teams, as a result, were promoted to the Third Division amidst celebratory scenes at the final whistle.

The Grecians had to make some pretty long journeys to fulfil fixtures at places like Barrow, Carlisle, Darlington and Workington as Graham well remembers.

"We went everywhere by coach. When Frank Broome had been manager at the club we used the train to get to games, but now we went by road, and this was before the days of the motorway.

"I could never sleep on a coach, and used to sit at the front and look at the road ahead of us. On return trips we reached Gloucester on the A38 and I recall thinking only three hours to go before we get to Exeter!

"The journeys may have been very long, but we had a good group of players, with Curtis, Smyth and Thorne being a good laugh to be with."

Graham said that apart form the promotion dinner and reception that the players and staff attended, Hughes Garage of Exeter, gave the players the use of two cars, free of charge, to be shared between them for a week - a Ford Corsair and a Ford Zodiac.

Statistics 1963/4

EXETER CITY FIRST TEAM FIXTURES; RESULTS; ATTENDANCES; GOALSCORERS

Date	Opponent	H/A	Result	Att.	Goalscorers
Aug 24	Bradford City	A	2-1	4,668	Henderson 2
Aug 26	Carlisle United	A	0-3	6,454	
Aug 31	Lincoln City	H	0-0	5,449	
Sep 4	Oxford United (FLC1)	H	1-0	5,688	Cochrane
Sep 7	Gillingham	A	0-0	8,381	
Sep 11	Carlisle United	H	1-0	5,671	Curtis
Sep 14	Southport	H	1-1	5,335	Curtis
Sep 18	Aldershot	A	1-0	7,603	Henderson
Sep 21	Doncaster Rovers	H	3-1	5,775	Henderson 2, Curtis
Sep 25	Hull City (FLC2)	A	0-1	9,313	
Sep 28	Hartlepools United	A	1-1	2,391	Harvey
Oct 2	Aldershot	H	0-0	7,007	
Oct 5	Darlington	H	1-1	5,965	Curtis
Oct 9	Halifax Town	H	0-0	7,317	
Oct 12	Chester	A	0-2	6,966	
Oct 14	Halifax Town	A	0-2	3,760	
Oct 19	York City	H	1-0	5,549	Smyth
Oct 23	Tranmere Rovers	H	5-0	5,701	Phoenix, Mitchell, Curtis, Henderson, Rees
Oct 26	Barrow	A	1-1	3,214	Harvey (pen)
Oct 28	Tranmere Rovers	A	1-2	5,471	Harvey (pen)
Nov 2	Rochdale	H	0-1	6,249	
Nov 9	Oxford United	A	2-0	7,185	Curtis, Banks
Nov 16	Shrewsbury Town (FAC1)	H	2-1	7,232	Curtis, Anderson
Nov 23	Newport County	A	1-0	3,339	Banks
Nov 29	Stockport County	H	2-0	7,058	Rees, Banks
Dec 7	Bristol City (FAC2)	H	0-2	15,077	
Dec 14	Bradford City	H	4-1	5,566	Banks, Mitchell, Grace, Ellam (og)
Dec 21	Lincoln City	A	1-1	3,673	Grace
Dec 26	Brighton & H.A.	A	2-1	10,250	Thorne, Banks
Dec 28	Brighton & H.A.	H	0-0	9,873	
Jan 4	Workington	H	2-1	7,286	Banks, Grace
Jan 11	Gillingham	H	0-0	10,905	
Jan 18	Southport	A	1-1	1,618	Banks
Jan 25	Bradford P.A.	A	2-3	6,273	Banks, Grace
Feb 1	Doncaster Rovers	A	0-1	8,083	
Feb 8	Hartlepools United	H	2-1	6,177	Banks, Rees
Feb 15	Darlington	A	1-1	2,647	Rees
Feb 22	Chester	H	3-0	6,589	Banks, Mitchell, Ley
Feb 29	York City	A	2-1	3,817	Banks 2
Mar 7	Barrow	H	0-0	5,891	
Mar 14	Rochdale	A	3-1	2,113	Thorne 2, Banks
Mar 21	Oxford United	H	3-2	6,602	Thorne, Curtis, Kyle (og)
Mar 27	Torquay United	H	0-0	16,141	
Mar 30	Torquay United	A	0-0	13,655	
Apr 4	Newport County	H	3-1	6,077	Banks 2, Harvey
Apr 11	Stockport County	A	0-0	2,773	
Apr 13	Chesterfield	A	1-0	4,442	Banks
Apr 18	Bradford P.A.	H	2-3	9,722	Harvey (pen), Rees
Apr 21	Chesterfield	H	6-1	9,449	Banks 2, Thorne 2, Curtis, Rees
Apr 25	Workington	A	0-0	8,600	
Apr 28	Plymouth Argyle (DPB Final)	H	4-0	8,141	Thorne 3, Banks

EXETER CITY RESERVE TEAM FIXTURES; RESULTS: SCORERS

Date	Opponent	H/A	Result	Scorers
Aug 24	Portland United	H	5-2	Redwood 2, Williams, Ley, Own-goal
Aug 28	Bridgwater Town	H	0-2	
Aug 31	Chippenham Town	A	0-1	
Sep 7	Weymouth	H	4-4	Ley 2, Redwood, Riding
Sep 14	Salisbury City	A	1-3	Not known
Sep 18	Yeovil Town	H	4-1	Spiers, Stuckey, Symington, Riding
Sep 21	Bath City	A	2-2	Spiers, Redwood
Sep 25	Yeovil Town	A	1-1	Spiers
Sep 28	Weston-Super-Mare	H	0-1	
Oct 5	Bridport	A	2-2	Redwood, Own goal
Oct 9	Torquay United	A	2-5	Redwood, Edgar
Oct 12	Taunton Town	A	5-0	Northcott 3, Redwood, Edgar
Oct 19	Glastonbury	A	4-4	Redwood, Ley, Stuckey, Riding
Oct 26	Poole Town	H	1-2	Riding
Nov 2	Weston-Super-Mare	A	0-2	
Nov 9	Barnstaple Town	H	0-3	
Nov 16	Portland United	A	3-4	Rutley, Stuckey, Redwood
Nov 23	Welton Rovers	H	1-3	Ley
Nov 30	Bristol City	A	3-3	Spiers 3
Dec 14	Weymouth	A	1-4	Spiers
Dec 21	Salisbury City	H	2-2	Riding, Henderson
Dec 26	Bristol City	H	1-4	Spiers
Dec 28	Barnstaple Town	A	0-3	
Jan 4	Minehead	A	0-2	
Jan 11	Frome Town	A	1-1	Howells
Jan 18	Bridport	H	2-1	Riding, Rutley
Jan 25	Taunton Town	H	3-1	Riding, Quarrington, Curtis
Feb 1	Glastonbury	H	6-2	Riding 5, Spiers
Feb 8	Andover	A	1-3	Ley
Feb 15	Torquay United	H	2-2	Riding, Curtis
Feb 22	Dorchester Town	A	0-7	
Feb 29	Minehead	H	1-1	Redwood
Mar 4	Bristol City	H	0-4	
Mar 7	Poole Town	A	4-0	Riding 3, Welsh
Mar 11	Dorchester Town	H	1-1	Curtis
Mar 14	Andover	H	2-2	Redwood, Riding
Mar 27	Bideford	A	0-2	
Mar 28	Frome Town	H	2-2	Gerrard, Ley
Mar 30	Bideford	H	0-2	
Apr 4	Welton Rovers	A	1-3	Redwood
Apr 11	Bath City	H	3-3	Riding 2, Edgar
Apr 25	Chippenham Town	H	1-1	Symington

The home fixture against Bristol City on 26th December was abandoned due to fog.

FIRST TEAM LEAGUE APPEARANCES
Anderson 46; Harvey 46; Barnett 45; Rees 45; Smyth 44; MacDonald 42; Mitchell 38; Curtis 32; Grace 32; Banks 28; Thorne 24; Henderson 22; Phoenix 15; Ley 14; Hancock 9; Patrick 7; Edgar 6; Spiers 5; Cochrane 2; Rutley 2; Northcott 1; Parkhill 1.

FIRST TEAM LEAGUE GOALSCORERS
Banks 18; Curtis 9; Henderson 6; Rees 6; Thorne 6; Harvey 5; Grace 4; Mitchell 3; Ley 1; Phoenix 1; Smyth 1;

FIRST TEAM F.A. CUP APPEARANCES
Anderson 2; Barnett 2; Curtis 2; Grace 2; Harvey 2; MacDonald 2; Mitchell 2; Northcott 2; Phoenix 2; Rees 2; Smyth 2;

FIRST TEAM F.A. CUP GOALSCORERS
Anderson 1; Curtis 1.

FIRST TEAM FOOTBALL LEAGUE CUP APPEARANCES
Anderson 2; Barnett 2; Grace 2; Henderson 2; MacDonald 2; Mitchell 2; Harvey 2; Rees 2; Smyth 2; Cochrane 1; Curtis 1; Ley 1; Redwood 1.

FIRST TEAM FOOTBALL LEAGUE CUP GOALSCORERS
Cochrane 1.

FIRST TEAM DEVON PROFESSIONAL BOWL APPEARANCES
Banks 1; Barnett 1; Curtis 1; Hancock 1; Harvey 1; MacDonald 1; Mitchell 1; Rees 1; Smyth 1; Thorne 1.

FIRST TEAM DEVON PROFESSIONAL BOWL GOALSCORERS
Thorne 3; Banks 1.

LEAGUE ATTENDANCES:
Highest at St James' Park: 16.141 v Torquay United, 27th March 1964
Lowest at St James' Park: 5,335 v Southport, 14th September 1963.

Highest away attendance: 13,655 v Torquay United, 30th March 1964.
Lowest away attendance: 1,618 v Southport, 18th January 1964.

Average League attendance for season at St James' Park: 7,291.

FINAL TABLES 1963/4

DIVISION ONE	P	W	D	L	F	A	W	D	L	F	A	PTS
Liverpool	42	16	0	5	60	18	10	5	6	32	27	57
Manchester United	42	15	3	3	54	19	8	4	9	36	43	53
Everton	42	14	4	3	53	26	7	6	8	31	38	52
Tottenham Hotspur	42	13	3	5	54	31	9	4	8	43	50	51
Chelsea	42	12	3	6	36	24	8	7	6	36	32	50
Sheffield Wednesday	42	15	3	3	50	24	4	8	9	34	43	49
Blackburn Rovers	42	10	4	7	44	28	8	6	7	45	37	46
Arsenal	42	10	7	4	56	37	7	4	10	34	45	45
West Bromwich Albion	42	14	3	4	46	23	3	7	11	25	41	44
Burnley	42	9	6	6	43	35	7	5	9	27	26	43
Leicester City	42	9	4	8	33	27	7	7	7	28	31	43
Sheffield United	42	10	6	5	35	22	6	5	10	26	42	43
Nottingham Forest	42	9	5	7	34	24	7	4	10	30	44	41
West Ham United	42	8	7	6	45	38	6	5	10	24	36	40
Fulham	42	11	8	2	45	23	2	5	14	13	42	39
Wolves	42	6	9	6	36	34	6	6	9	34	46	39
Stoke City	42	9	6	6	49	33	5	4	12	28	45	38
Blackpool	42	8	6	7	26	29	5	3	13	26	44	35
Aston Villa	42	8	6	7	35	29	3	6	12	27	42	34
Birmingham City	42	7	7	7	33	32	4	0	17	21	60	29
Bolton Wanderers	42	6	5	10	30	35	4	3	14	18	45	28
Ipswich Town	42	9	3	9	38	45	0	4	17	18	76	25

DIVISION TWO	P	W	D	L	F	A	W	D	L	F	A	PTS
Leeds United	42	12	9	0	35	16	19	6	3	36	18	63
Sunderland	42	16	3	2	47	13	9	8	4	34	24	61
Preston North End	42	13	7	1	37	14	10	3	8	42	40	56
Charlton Athletic	42	11	4	6	44	30	8	6	7	32	40	48
Southampton	42	13	3	5	69	32	6	6	9	31	41	47
Manchester City	42	12	4	5	50	27	6	6	9	34	39	46
Rotherham United	42	14	3	4	52	26	5	4	12	38	52	45
Newcastle United	42	14	2	5	49	26	6	3	12	25	43	45
Portsmouth	42	9	7	5	46	34	7	4	10	33	36	43
Middlesbrough	42	14	4	3	47	16	1	7	13	20	36	41
Northampton Town	42	10	2	9	35	31	6	7	8	23	29	41
Huddersfield Town	42	11	4	6	31	25	4	6	11	26	39	40
Derby County	42	10	6	5	34	27	4	5	12	22	40	39
Swindon Town	42	11	5	5	39	24	3	5	13	18	45	38
Cardiff City	42	10	7	4	31	27	4	3	14	25	54	38
Leyton Orient	42	8	6	7	32	32	5	4	12	22	40	36
Norwich City	42	9	7	5	43	30	2	6	13	21	50	35
Bury	42	8	5	8	35	36	5	4	12	22	37	35
Swansea Town	42	11	4	6	44	26	1	5	15	19	48	33
Plymouth Argyle	42	6	8	7	26	32	2	8	11	19	35	32
Grimsby Town	42	6	7	8	28	34	3	7	11	19	41	32
Scunthorpe United	42	8	8	5	30	25	2	2	17	22	57	30

DIVISION THREE	P	W	D	L	F	A	W	D	L	F	A	PTS
Coventry City	46	14	7	2	62	32	8	9	6	36	29	60
Crystal Palace	46	17	4	2	38	14	6	10	7	35	37	60
Watford	46	16	6	1	57	28	7	6	10	22	31	58
Bournemouth	46	17	4	2	47	15	7	4	12	32	43	56
Bristol City	46	13	7	3	52	24	7	8	8	32	40	55
Reading	46	15	5	3	49	26	6	5	12	30	36	52
Mansfield Town	46	15	8	0	51	20	5	3	15	25	42	51
Hull City	46	11	9	3	45	27	5	8	10	28	41	49
Oldham Athletic	46	13	3	7	44	35	7	5	11	29	35	48
Peterborough United	46	13	6	4	52	27	5	5	13	23	43	47
Shrewsbury Town	46	13	6	4	43	19	5	5	13	30	61	47
Bristol Rovers	46	9	6	8	52	34	10	2	11	39	45	46
Port Vale	46	13	6	4	35	13	3	8	12	18	36	46
Southend	46	9	10	4	42	26	6	5	12	35	52	45
QPR	46	13	4	6	47	34	5	5	13	29	44	45
Brentford	46	11	4	8	54	36	4	10	9	33	44	44
Colchester United	46	10	8	5	45	26	2	11	10	25	42	43
Luton Town	46	12	2	9	42	41	4	8	11	22	39	42
Walsall	46	7	9	7	34	35	6	5	12	25	41	40
Barnsley	46	9	9	5	34	29	3	6	14	34	65	39
Millwall	46	9	4	10	33	29	5	6	12	20	38	38
Crewe Alexandra	46	10	5	8	29	26	1	7	15	21	51	34
Wrexham	46	9	4	10	50	42	4	2	17	25	65	32
Notts County	46	7	8	8	29	26	2	1	20	16	66	27

DIVISION FOUR	P	W	D	L	F	A	W	D	L	F	A	PTS
Gillingham	46	16	7	0	37	10	7	7	9	22	20	60
Carlisle United	46	17	3	3	70	20	8	7	8	43	38	60
Workington	46	15	6	2	46	19	9	5	9	30	33	59
Exeter City	46	12	9	2	39	14	8	9	6	23	23	58
Braford City	46	15	3	5	45	24	10	3	10	31	38	56
Torquay United	46	16	6	1	60	20	4	5	14	20	34	51
Tranmere Rovers	46	12	4	7	46	20	8	7	8	39	43	51
Brighton	46	13	3	7	45	22	6	9	8	26	30	50
Aldershot	46	15	3	5	58	28	4	7	12	25	50	48
Halifax Town	46	14	4	5	47	28	3	10	10	30	49	48
Lincoln City	46	15	2	6	49	31	4	7	12	18	44	47
Chester	46	17	3	3	47	18	2	5	16	18	42	46
Bradford (PA)	46	13	5	5	50	34	5	4	14	25	47	45
Doncaster Rovers	46	11	8	4	46	23	4	4	15	24	52	42
Newport County	46	12	3	8	35	24	5	5	13	29	49	42
Chesterfield	46	8	9	6	29	27	7	3	13	28	44	42
Stockport County	46	12	7	4	32	19	3	5	15	18	49	42
Oxford United	46	10	7	6	37	27	4	6	13	22	36	41
Darlington	46	8	9	6	40	37	6	3	14	26	56	40
Rochdale	46	9	8	6	36	24	3	7	13	20	35	39
Southport	46	12	6	5	42	29	3	3	17	21	59	39
York City	46	9	3	11	29	26	5	4	14	23	40	35
Hartlepools United	46	8	7	8	30	36	4	2	17	24	57	33
Barrow	46	4	10	9	30	36	2	8	13	21	57	30

CITY'S OPPONENTS 1963/4

League Appearances and Goals

ALDERSHOT		Apps	Gls
Burton	A	40	11
Carson	A	1	
Chamberlain	P	12	
Devereux	A	24	
Fogg	R	43	21
Henry	G	24	
Jones	D	46	
Kearns	P	20	6
Mulgrew	T	44	
Norris	G	2	2
Palethorpe	C	40	3
Priscott	A	29	16
Renwick	R	40	1
Smith	J	28	
Stepney	R	29	4
Thomas	R	29	
Towers	E	28	13
Tyer	A	15	1
Woan	A	12	4
Own Goals			1

BRADFORD CITY		Apps	Gls
Blacker	J	2	
Ellam	R	46	1
Fisher	J	46	
Fletcher	G	8	1
Green	H	44	29
Hall	J	31	3
Harland	S	37	5
Hellawell	J	25	7
Kelly	B	46	
Price	T	36	15
Redfearn	B	7	2
Sawyer	B	6	1
Smith	M	42	
Storton	S	1	
Stowell	B	29	
Thorpe	A	30	6
Tong	R	14	1
Webster	J	15	1
Wragg	P	41	1
Own Goals			3

BARROW		Apps	Gls
Ackerley	E	38	10
Anderson	T	11	3
Arrowsmith	B	45	1
Barratt	L	8	
Brennan	R	14	3
Brown	G	4	2
Cahill	T	35	
Caine	B	45	
Clark	B	34	
Corkhill	R	6	
Darwin	G	16	5
Eddy	K	24	
Hale	R	35	2
Howard	S	31	4
Kemp	J	19	4
Lodge	G	6	
Maddison	J	39	3
Murray	T	3	
O'Neil	N	35	3
Smyth	M	1	
Thomson	T	28	10
Wearmouth	M	22	
Whitelaw	G	7	
Own Goals			1

BRADFORD (PARK AVENUE)

		Apps	Gls
Atkinson	C	42	3
Bird	R	44	14
Blackhall	S	1	
Burns	E	18	3
Church	G	4	
Cook	M	13	2
Dine	J	13	
Evans	R	13	5
Flynn	P	28	2
Fryatt	J	26	11
Gebbie	R	10	
Gould	G	2	
Hannigan	J	22	5
Hardie	J	23	
Hector	K	46	17
Anson	P	2	
Jones	K	39	
Lawrie	S	9	4
Lightowler	G	11	
McCalman	D	43	1
Scoular	J	20	
Spratt	T	36	6
Thomas	G	26	
Walker	J	15	
Own Goals			2

CARLISLE UNITED

		Apps	Gls
Brayton	B	15	6
Cldwell	T	46	
Davies	E	38	10
Dean	J	12	
Evans	J	15	16
Forrest	W	3	
Garrett	J	1	
Goodall	B	1	
Johnstone	E	5	1
Kirkup	F	37	6
Livingstone	J	30	20
Lornie	J	4	
Marsden	J	14	
McConnell	P	44	7
McIlmoyle	H	45	39
McNichol	R	1	
Neil	H	45	
Oliphant	D	6	
Passmoor	T	22	
Ross	J	34	
Taylor	S	36	2
Thompson	R	42	1
Twentyman	G	10	
Own Goals		10	5

BRIGHTON

		Apps	Gls
Baxter	R	11	2
Bertolini	J	30	4
Burtenshaw	S	33	1
Cassidy	W	29	6
Collins	J	46	12
Cooper	J	21	4
Donnelly	P	8	2
Fitch	B	1	
Gall	N	41	
Gilbert	P	1	
Goodchild	J	42	14
Gould	W	18	3
Healer	A	3	1
Jackson	A	6	
Jennings	R	29	
Knight	P	2	
McGonigal	R	21	
Powney	B	25	
Sanders	A	41	
Smith	J	13	6
Turner	D	23	2
Upton	R	25	
Waites	G	8	
Webber	K	29	13
Own Goals		1	1

170

CHESTER		Apps	Gls
Adams	F	8	
Bades	B	15	1
Barton	C	6	
Bennion	S	20	3
Butler	J	46	
Corbishley	C	41	7
Currie	J	2	
Evans	G	25	
Evans	J	27	
Fitzgerald	P	1	
Fleming	B	18	
Haddock	A	12	
Hauser	P	22	
Humes	J	22	3
Jones	R	14	
Lee	G	27	7
McGill	J	7	
McGowan	G	3	
Metcalf	M	24	8
Molyneaux	J	23	
Morris	E	24	8
Pritchard	A	2	
Read	D	32	4
Reeves	D	32	
Starkey	M	21	
Talbot	G	32	23
Own Goals			1

CHESTERFIELD		Apps	Gls
Armstrong	I	7	
Beresford	W	13	1
Beresford	P	7	3
Blakey	D	43	1
Clarke	G	35	3
Duncan	G	36	4
Frear	B	31	10
Frost	B	29	6
Hinton	R	1	
Holmes	A	30	1
Hughes	E	37	
Lovie	J	20	
McQuarrie	A	17	5
Meredith	J	35	1
Osborne	J	23	
Poole	R	8	1
Powell	R	23	
Rackstraw	C	46	15
Scott	J	5	
Sears	G	41	1
Whitham	T	19	2
Own Goals			3

DARLINGTON		Apps	Gls
Allison	K	13	15
Atkinson	T	23	
Burbeck	R	18	1
Curley	W	8	
Duffy	J	10	1
Greener	R	42	1
Heaviside	J	2	
Henderson	B	27	1
Hirt	R	17	
Lawton	J	40	14
Maltby	I	36	10
McGeachie	G	15	3
O'Neill	J	3	
Oliver	E	2	
Penman	C	24	
Peverell	J	34	
Potter	J	19	1
Rayment	J	31	4
Robson	J	14	
Robson	L	39	6
Smith	W	26	7
Storton	S	15	
Weddell	R	13	2
Whitehead	R	17	

DONCASTER ROVERS		Apps	Gls	GILLINGHAM		Apps	Gls
Billings	J	3		Arnott	J	43	
Booth	C	43	23	Ballagher	J	17	4
Broadbent	A	39	5	Burgess	M	46	1
Conwell	A	16		Campbell	D	1	
Crompton	D	23		Farrell	A	45	1
Downie	M	7		Francis	G	16	7
Fairhurst	J	9		Gibbs	B	46	17
Hale	A	44	20	Godfrey	P	13	2
Haspell	A	1		Hdson	G	36	1
Hellewell	K	6		Hunt	D	43	3
Jeffrey	A	20	4	Meredith	J	11	
Lambton	G	6		Moss	R	2	
McMinn	R	1		Newman	R	37	11
Meadows	R	17		Pulley	G	31	6
Moore	B	1		Ridley	J	7	2
Myers	J	20		Simpson	L	46	
Nibloe	J	20	2	Stacey	T	12	
Potter	F	33		Stringfellow	P	25	
Raine	D	39	2	Taylor	R	1	
Ripley	S	36	4	Waldock	R	6	
Robinson	B	37	5	White	J	11	1
Taylor	F	17	3	Yeo	B	11	2
Westlake	B	5	1	Own Goals			1
White	R	43					
Windross	D	20	1				
Own Goals			1				

HALIFAX TOWN		Apps	Gls	HARTLEPOOLS UNITED		Apps	Gls
Arnell	A	14	6	Atkinson	C	17	
Bartlett	F	21	4	Bilcliff	R	41	
Bingley	W	32	1	Bradley	W	38	5
Brier	J	4		Brown	J	22	5
Carlin	W	41	21	Burlison	T	31	1
Downsborough	P	42		Cunningham	K	2	
Fidler	D	38	10	Fogarty	A	28	5
Field	A	4	1	Francis	T	14	3
Granger	M	1		Fraser	A	44	2
Harrison	E	46	5	Hamilton	H	17	4
Heys	M	1		Hinccliffe	J	41	5
Jackson	D	35	1	Hinshelwood	W	17	3
Kelly	J	3		Johnson	K	23	3
Richardson	G	18		Lithgo	G	23	6
Roscoe	P	40		McCubbin	R	2	
Russell	M	20		McLean	J	23	3
South	A	31		Morrell	R	11	
Tait	B	2		Oakley	N	33	
Taylor	A	31	7	Simpkins	K	13	
Twist	F	40	5	Stonehouse	D	29	
Westlake	B	20	11	Thompson	P	22	8
Wilkinson	S	2		Walls	D	2	
Worthington	D	20	4	Wilkie	D	13	
Own Goals			1	Own Goals			1

LINCOLN CITY

		Apps	Gls
Bannister	N	11	3
Bracewell	K	7	1
Campbell	J	22	4
Carling	T	46	
Drysdale	B	4	
Fell	J	20	1
Gedney	C	1	
Green	N	9	
Grummitt	J	4	
Heward	B	45	2
Holmes	R	44	2
Houghton	H	24	14
Jackson	R	5	
Jones	A	40	
Jones	J	1	
Linnecor	A	29	8
Milner	J	29	2
Moore	J	11	3
Morton	A	44	18
Neal	R	38	4
Punter	B	7	
Roone	R	14	1
Smith	J	43	
Spears	A	2	
Stanton	B	1	
Wilkinson	B	5	3
Own Goals			1

ROCHDALE

		Apps	Gls
Aspden	J	39	
Burgin	E	40	
Cairns	R	23	7
Hardman	J	5	
Hepton	S	36	
Jones	S	6	
Kerry	D	12	4
MacKenzie	D	18	5
Martin	G	8	1
Miulbur	S	44	1
Morton	G	40	9
Phoenix	P	4	
Richrdson	J	33	11
Storf	D	45	4
Taylor	B	15	
Thompson	J	45	4
Watson	D	25	7
Wells	W	8	
Winton	G	38	
Wragg	D	22	2
Own Goal			1

NEWPORT COUNTY

		Apps	Gls
Bird	J	35	
Bonson	J	42	25
Frowen	J	22	
Hill	L	25	1
Hunt	R	39	10
Kear	M	6	
Pring	K	27	3
Rathbone	G	45	
Reece	G	3	
Reynolds	G	11	3
Rowland	J	45	1
Sheffield	L	35	12
Smith	G	41	6
Walters	G	40	
Weare	L	46	
Webster	C	23	3
Williams	D	21	

OXFORD UNITED

		Apps	Gls
Atkinson	R	41	3
Beavon	C	45	
Bowstead	P	3	
Bryan	P	1	
Buck	A	1	
Calder	W	25	9
Cassidy	J	5	
Colfar	R	1	1
Cornwall	K	15	5
Evans	B	5	2
Fahy	J	1	
Fearnley	H	23	
Harrington	C	43	7
Hartland	M	10	3
Havenhand	K	7	1
Higgins	P	4	
Houghton	H	11	1
Jones	A	46	2
Knight	P	39	7
Kyle	M	45	
Longbottom	A	30	12
Love	J	2	
Quatermain	P	39	
Richard	M	3	
Rouse	RV	20	
Shuker	J	12	
Willey	A	29	5
Own Goals			1

174

SOUTHPORT

		Apps	Gls
Ambler	R	11	
Beanland	A	44	1
Blore	R	19	6
Brookes	C	20	2
Brown	G	4	1
Cairns	K	39	
Dagger	J	43	3
Darvell	R	26	
Harris	A	8	
Latham	D	22	
Peat	W	38	3
Phoenix	P	10	
Rollo	J	38	
Russell	A	27	6
Rutherford	W	11	1
Scott	R	3	
Senior	P	2	
Shepherd	J	13	6
Spence	A	46	27
Tighe	T	36	3
Wallace	J	46	
Own Goals			4

STOCKPORT COUNTY

		Apps	Gls
Beighton	G	44	
Bircumshaw	P	17	4
Collins	J	7	
Cuthbert	E	34	
Davenport	C	12	3
Davock	M	28	6
Eckersall	M	8	
Evans	J	30	9
France	A	30	8
Hodder	K	3	
Johnston	D	26	
Lea	H	2	
McDonnell	C	25	
Parry	C	40	
Porteous	T	36	1
Ricketts	G	46	3
Ryden	H	38	9
Stainsby	J	5	
Ward	D	13	
Watt	J	38	3
Wylie	J	44	1
Own Goals			3

TORQUAY UNITED

		Apps	Gls
Adlington	T	40	
Allen	G	40	
Anderson	P	37	10
Austin	J	22	
Balsom	C	4	
Barnsley	G	6	
Bettany	C	36	
Cox	G	16	2
Hancock	D	23	2
Handley	B	10	3
Jenkins	R	37	7
Northcott`	T	38	10
Pym	E	35	9
Richardson	R	2	
Rossiter	J	7	
Smith	J	28	1
Spencer	R	19	
Stubbs	R	34	24
Swindells	J	18	6
Tolchard	J	1	
Webb	R	12	3
Williams	J	19	
Wolstenholme	J	22	
Own Goals			3

TRANMERE ROVERS

		Apps	Gls
Billington	S	34	
Campbell	L	43	4
Coleman	A	7	
Conroy	R	44	
Dyson	J	45	26
Edwards	M	26	1
Evans	B	12	5
Gubbins	R	16	1
Heath	J	24	
Hickson	D	12	2
Jackson	P	24	2
Jones	L	37	15
King	A	5	
King	I	42	1
Leyland	H	22	
Manning	J	30	20
McDonnell	C	5	2
Oxtoby	R	5	
Pritchard	J	5	
Roberts	R	39	1
Sinclair	R	1	
Wilkinson	G	3	
Wilson	J	25	
Own Goals			5

WORKINGTON		Apps	Gls	YORK CITY		Apps	Gls
Brown	R	44		Ashworth	J	24	
Burkinshaw	K	44	1	Baker	G	33	5
Carr	D	39	21	Barmby	J	1	
Chapman	J	2		Boyes	K	9	
Commons	M	7	3	Forgan	T	20	
Furphy	K	44	1	Fountain	J	13	
Hopper	W	37	13	Goldie	J	22	7
Johnston	A	44		Gould	W	25	6
Lowes	B	21	11	Heron	T	46	3
Lumsden	I	46	1	Hoggart	D	6	1
Martin	G	45	10	Jackson	C	38	
Middlemass	C	7		Lang	M	12	2
Moran	J	46	7	Meechan	D	6	
Morton	G	2		Moor	A	24	
Ogilvie	J	2		Peyton	N	35	4
Ower	I	46		Popely	P	8	
Peacock	E	1		Rudd	W	46	7
Timmins	A	5		Scott	J	21	3
Watson	P	24	6	Scott	M	19	
Own Goals			2	Wealthall	B	32	
				Wilkinson	N	27	10
				Wolstenholme	I	2	
				Woods	A	37	2
				Own Goals			2

F.A. CUP 1963/4

Third Round

West Ham United v Charlton Athletic	3-0
Leicester City v Leyton Orient	2-3
Aston Villa v Aldershot	0-0, 1-2
Swindon Town v Manchester City	2-1
Burnley v Rotherham United	1-1, 3-2
Newport County v Sheffield Wednesday	3-2
Tottenham Hotspur v Chelsea	1-1, 0-2
Plymouth Argyle v Huddersfield Town	0-1
Sunderland v Northampton Town	2-0
Doncaster Rovers v Bristol City	2-2, 0-2
Cardiff City v Leeds United	0-1
Hull City v Everton	1-1, 1-2
Scunthorpe United v Barnsley	2-2, 2-3
Yeovil Town v Bury	0-2
Southampton v Manchester United	2-3
Bristol Rovers v Norwich City	2-1
Ipswich Town v Oldham Athletic	6-3
Stoke City v Portsmouth	4-1
Lincoln City v Sheffield United	0-4
Swansea Town v Barrow	4-1
West Bromwich Albion v Blackpool	2-2, 1-0
Arsenal v Wolves	2-1
Liverpool v Derby County	5-0
Birmingham City v Port Vale	1-2
Oxford United v Chesterfield	1-0
Brentford v Middlesbrough	2-1
Blackburn Rovers v Grimsby Town	4-0
Fulham v Luton Town	4-1
Newcastle United v Bedford Town	1-2
Carlisle United v Queen's Park Rangers	2-0
Bath City v Bolton Wanderers	1-1, 0-3
Nottingham Forest v Preston North End	0-0, 0-1

Fourth Round

West Ham United v Leyton Orient	1-1, 3-0
Aldershot v Swindon Town	1-2
Burnley v Newport County	2-1
Chelsea v Huddersfield Town	1-2
Sunderland v Bristol City	6-1
Leeds United v Everton	1-1, 0-2
Barnsley v Bury	2-1
Manchester United v Bristol Rovers	4-1
Ipswich Town v Stoke City	1-1, 0-1
Sheffield United v Swansea Town	1-1, 0-4
West Bromwich Albion v Arsenal	3-3, 0-2
Liverpool v Port Vale	0-0, 2-1
Oxford United v Brentford	2-2, 2-1
Blackburn Rovers v Fulham	2-0
Bedford Town v Carlisle United	0-3
Bolton Wanderers v Preston North End	2-2, 1-2

Fifth Round

West Ham United v Swindon Town	3-1
Burnley v Huddersfield Town	3-0
Sunderland v Everton	3-1
Barnsley v Manchester United	0-4
Stoke City v Swansea Town	2-2, 0-2
Arsenal v Liverpool	0-1
Oxford United v Blackburn Rovers	3-1
Carlisle United v Preston North End	0-1

Sixth Round

West Ham United v Burnley	3-2
Sunderland v Manchester United	3-3, 2-2
	1-5
Swansea Town v Liverpool	2-1
Oxford United v Preston North End	1-2

Semi Finals

West Ham United v Manchester United	3-1
(at Hillsborough)	
Swnsea Town v Preston North End	1-2
(at Villa Park)	

Final

West Ham United v Preston North End	3-2
(at Wembley)	

West Ham: Standen, Bond, Burkett, Bovingdon, Brown, Moore, Brabrook, Boyce, Byrne, Hurst, Sissons
Preston: Kelly, Ross, Smith, Lawton, Singleton, Kendall, Wilson, Ashworth, Dawson, Spavin, Holden

0-1	10 mins	Holden
1-1	12 mins	Sissons
1-2	40 mins	Dawson
2-2	52 mins	Hurst
3-2	90+2 mins	Boyce

Football League Cup 1963/4

First Round

Aldershot v Queen's Park Rangers	3-1
Bradford (PA) v Bradford City	7-3
Carlisle United v Crewe Alexandra	3-2
Chesterfield v Halifax Town	0-1
Darlington v Barnsley	2-2, 2-6
Doncaster Rovers v York City	0-0, 0-3
Gillingham v Bristol City	4-2
Lincoln City v Hartlepools United	3-2
Mansfield Town v Watford	2-1
Newport County v Millwall	3-4
Oldham Athletic v Workington	3-5
Oxford United v Exeter City	0-1
Reading v Brentford	1-1, 0-2
Rochdale v Chester	1-1, 5-2
Shrewsbury Town v Bristol Rovers	1-1, 2-6
Southport v Barrow	2-1
Torquay United v Brighton and H Albion	1-2
Tranmere Rovers v Stockport County	2-0

Second Round

Aston Villa v Barnsley	3-1
Blackpool v Charlton Athletic	7-1
Bradford (PA) v Middlesbrough	2-2, 3-2
Brentford v Bournemouth	0-0, 0-2
Brighton and H Albion v Northampton T	1-1, 2-3
Bristol Rovers v Crystal Palace	2-0
Cardiff City v Wrexham	2-2, 1-1
	0-3
Colchester United v Fulham	5-3
Gillingham v Bury	3-0
Grimsby Town v Rotherham United	1-3
Halifax Town v Rochdale	4-2
Hull City v Exeter City	1-0
Ipswich Town v Walsall	0-0, 0-1
Leeds United v Mansfield Town	5-1
Leicester City v Aldershot	2-0
Luton Town v Coventry City	3-4
Manchester City v Carlisle United	2-0
Millwall v Peterborough United	3-2
Newcastle United v Preston North End	3-0
Norwich City v Birmingham City	2-0
Notts County v Blackburn Rovers	2-1
Plymouth Argyle v Huddersfield Town	2-2, 3-3
	1-2
Portsmouth v Derby County	3-2
Scunthorpe United v Stoke City	2-2, 3-3
	0-1
Sheffield United v Bolton Wanderers	1-2

Southend United v Port Vale	2-1
Swansea Town v Sunderland	3-1
Swindon Town v Chelsea	3-0
Tranmere Rovers v Southampton	2-0
West Ham United v Leyton Orient	2-1
Workington v Southport	3-0
York City v Lincoln City	1-1, 0-2

Third Round

Aston Villa v West Ham United	0-2
Halifax Town Walsall	2-0
Hull City v Manchester City	0-3
Swindon Town v Southend United	3-0
Tranmere Rovers v Leicester City	1-2
Leeds United v Swansea Town	2-0
Bristol Rovers v Gillingham	1-1, 1-3
Colchester United v Northampton Town	4-1
Millwall v Lincoln City	1-1, 1-2
Rotherham United v Coventry City	4-2
Workington v Huddersfield Town	1-0
Wrexham v Portsmouth	3-5
Notts County v Bradford (PA)	3-2
Stoke City v Bolton Wanderers	3-0
Norwich City v Blackpool	1-0
Bournemouth v Newcastle United	2-1

Fourth Round

Notts County v Portsmouth	3-2
Swindon Town v West Ham United	3-3, 1-4
Workington v Colchester United	2-1
Halifax Town v Norwich City	1-7
Leicester City v Gillingham	3-1
Manchester City v Leeds United	3-1
Stoke City v Bournemouth	2-1
Rotherham United v Millwall	5-2

Fifth Round

West Ham v Workington	6-0
Norwich City v Leicester City	1-1, 1-2
Notts County v Manchester City	0-1
Stoke City v Rotherham	3-2

Semi Finals

Stoke City v Manchester City	2-0, 0-1
Leicester City v West Ham United	4-3, 2-0

Final

Stoke City v Leicester City	1-1, 2-3

International Matches 1963/4

October	12	Wales v England	HIC	Cardiff	1-4
	23	England v Rest of the World	Fr	Wembley	2-1
November	20	England v Northern Ireland	HIC	Wembley	8-3
April	11	Scotland v England	HIC	Hampden	1-0
May	6	England v Uruguay	Fr	Wembley	2-1
	17	Portugal v England	Fr	Lisbon	3-4
	24	Republic of Ireland v England	Fr	Dublin	1-3
	27	USA v England	Fr	New York	1-10
	30	Brazil v England	Fr*	Rio de Janeiro	5-1
June	4	Portugal v England	Fr*	Sao Paulo	1-1
	6	Argentina v England	Fr*	Rio de Janeiro	1-0

* Matches to celebrate 50 Years of the Brazilian FA

Home International Championship Table

	P	W	D	L	F	A	PTS
England	3	2	0	1	12	4	4
Scotland	3	2	0	1	4	3	4
Northern Ireland	3	2	0	1	8	11	4
Wales	3	0	0	3	3	9	0

Players Capped 1963-4

Bobby Charlton	Manchester United	10
George Eastham	Arsenal	10
Bobby Moore	West Ham United	10
Maurice Norman	Tottenham Hotspur	10
Gordon Banks	Leicester City	9
Jimmy Greaves	Tottenham Hotspur	9
Gordon Milne	Liverpool	9
Ray Wilson	Huddersfield Town	9
Johnny Byrne	West Ham United	7
Terry Paine	Southampton	7
Peter Thompson	Liverpool	6
George Cohen	Fulham	5
Jimmy Armfield	Blackpool	4
Bobby Thomson	Wolves	4
Ron Flowers	Wolves	3
Roger Hunt	Liverpool	3
Bobby Smith	Tottenham Hotspur	3
Tony Waiters	Blackpool	2
Mike Bailey	Charlton Athletic	1
Fred Pickering	Everton	1